Generative
LEADERSHIP

Shaping New Futures for Today's Schools

KARL J. KLIMEK
ELSIE RITZENHEIN
KATHRYN D. SULLIVAN

Foreword by SENATOR JOHN H. GLENN

CORWIN PRESS
A SAGE Company
Thousand Oaks, CA 91320

For information:

Corwin Press
A SAGE Company
2455 Teller Road
Thousand Oaks,
   California 91320
www.corwinpress.com

SAGE Pvt. Ltd.
B 1/I 1 Mohan Cooperative
   Industrial Area
Mathura Road, New Delhi 110 044
India

SAGE Pvt. Ltd.
1 Oliver's Yard
55 City Road
London EC1Y 1SP
United Kingdom

SAGE Asia-Pacific Pte. Ltd.
33 Pekin Street #02-01
Far East Square
Singapore 048763

Printed in the United States of America.

Library of Congress Cataloging-in-Publication Data

Klimek, Karl J.
Generative leadership : shaping new futures for today's schools/
Karl J. Klimek, Elsie Ritzenhein, Kathryn D. Sullivan.
    p. cm.
Includes bibliographical references and index.
ISBN 978-1-4129-5301-6 (cloth)
ISBN 978-1-4129-5302-3 (pbk.)
   1. Educational leadership. 2. School management and
organization. I. Ritzenhein, Elsie. II. Sullivan, Kathryn D.
III. Title.

LB2805.K527 2008
371.2—dc22   2007045666

This book is printed on acid-free paper.

08   09   10   11   12   10 9 8 7 6 5 4 3 2

Acquisitions Editor:	Hudson Perigo
Editorial Assistant:	Lesley Blake
Production Editor:	Veronica Stapleton
Copy Editor:	Linda Gray
Typesetter:	C&M Digitals (P) Ltd.
Proofreader:	Gail Fay
Indexer:	Kirsten Kite
Cover Designer:	Michael Dubowe
Graphic Designer:	Monique Hahn

Contents

Foreword

At the beginning of the 20th century, American schools underwent profound changes as they adapted curricula and teaching practices to the demands of industrialization and a growing population. Now, eight years into a new century, our schools confront an even greater challenge: to achieve the systemic transformation needed to prepare our children well for the increasingly complex world they will enter. Countless studies, reports, and articles have been written on the mechanisms that can incentivize or compel the changes needed. Far fewer works have addressed the one element that is essential to any constructive and effective change: leadership.

What kind of leadership is needed to reshape our schools? Certainly not the type that focuses solely on assigning tasks, managing units of time, and verifying compliance. Management and audit tasks such as these have an important place in stewardship of our schools, but they are not the essential tasks of leadership. Our schools need leadership that challenges the imaginations of our students and teachers. They need leadership that can uncover the liberating opportunities concealed within daunting challenges—this is the defining ability of American genius. This is the "generative leadership" we come to understand so clearly in this powerful and concise volume.

Kathy Sullivan is one of the first people who comes to mind whenever I think of education or leadership, so it's no surprise to find her playing a central role in bringing this vital subject to the fore. She and her colleagues, Karl Klimek and Elsie Ritzenhein, have done a masterful job of synthesizing large bodies of complex work into an engaging and readable narrative that outlines the foundations of generative leadership. They follow this foundation with a variety of practical tools to help school leaders jump-start their leadership practice.

We typically think of teachers, principals, and superintendents as school leaders. In our country, however, parents and businesspeople, nonprofit executives and academics are also part of school leadership. This book can inform and potentially unite all these school leaders in the common cause of reshaping our schools for the challenges of this new century.

—Senator John H. Glenn

Preface

This book is the result of three independent learning journeys that intersected some years ago at a point of shared passion: the urgent imperative for change within American schools, given the vital role that good education plays in the future well-being of our children and our nation. We joined forces to speak from our collective experience as leader–educators about a different approach to leadership—one that we believe is urgently needed in our schools and school communities. Experience has taught each of us that this kind of leadership—generative leadership—unleashes energy, intelligence, and creativity from within the entire school and so opens new avenues for action. A vibrant, positive culture emerges, one in which deep learning and high achievement become norms for everybody. Imagine going to a school like that!

On the surface, we may seem an unlikely trio—a principal, a former assistant superintendent, a retired astronaut—and our professional paths are certainly quite different. But we have some important things in common. We all love teaching and learning, and we care deeply about the state of education today. Each of us has served in a variety of leadership roles, including teacher, pilot, school principal, military officer, orchestra conductor, and CEO. In organizations large and small, we have faced complex challenges, fierce scrutiny, multitudes of stakeholders, and severe consequences. We have watched the leaders who preceded us and have been given the usual leadership development opportunities offered by our universities and professional organizations. More often than not, we found that these didn't really help us make sense of or resolve the complex challenges

> Maybe people confronting complex challenges in other realms of human endeavor had learned some lessons that could be imported or adapted to our world of education.

confronting us. How come? Being curious types, we wondered if there weren't other ways to go about this. Maybe people confronting complex challenges in other realms of human endeavor had learned some lessons that could be imported or adapted to our world of education.

Propelled by these and other questions, each of us began our own journey of research and personal growth, largely in domains outside education. Every new bit of learning was tested in the crucible of our school or agency, our professional association or family. We discovered important knowledge and powerful principles in neurophysiology, social science, cognitive psychology, management consulting, and the natural and physical sciences. Through books, courses, and seminars, we enjoyed a rich discourse with theorists and practitioners who were seeking answers to the same questions on behalf of leaders in large corporations and national governments. Many of these provided gratifying confirmation of ideas and methods, even of the vocabulary that had already emerged through our own practice; all of them guided us to yet further inquiry.

Through all this exploration, we each arrived independently at some common conclusions. Leadership for these times—for today's schools—must go beyond the old methods, anchored as they are in simplistic machinelike representations of our world, our workplaces, and ourselves. Effective leadership for the 21st century needs to be more multidimensional. It must focus on relationships and interdependencies within every organization and work from a mental model of organizations as systems rather than as structures. Leadership must set creativity and intelligence free, not just control time and materials. It must welcome the involvement of many and tap the intelligence of all. Leaders must pose powerful questions rather than just impose directives. Powerful questions generate energy, focus inquiry, reveal hidden assumptions, and so open new possibilities for action. We need leaders who are proud to be continual learners and who see their main job as leading the collective learning of their organization. Our times call for leaders who give up some control in order to get collaboration, creativity, and the collective intelligence surrounding them. We need generative leaders.

> Leadership must set creativity and intelligence free, not just control time and materials.

Although many of these insights came from studies of corporations, they are not particular to one certain kind of organization or another. They are rooted in our human nature and in principles common to all living systems. This makes them transferable: Fundamental insights demonstrated in one setting can be applied in other human social settings, from a family to a corporation, from a nation to a school.

We were saddened to find that there hasn't been much transfer of these insights to school leadership. Thus arose the idea for a book tailored to active school leaders. We thought of it as a blend of basic primer and introductory field guide: a small, easy-to-read volume that gives school leaders a concise initial grounding in the foundational elements of generative leadership plus some basic tools to help them jump-start or expand their practice of it. That is the book you now hold in your hands.

This book is for anybody who touches the education of a child. From a generative perspective, this includes everybody in a school community—whether teacher, parent, relative, principal, janitor, stakeholder, or superintendent. All are individual elements of the living system of learning that our children depend on; each and every one shapes the system and affects all outcomes. We hope these pages help you see your school with new eyes and begin to work from that new view. We hope this book inspires you to start new conversations that transform how the people in your school come together to achieve deep learning for the entire school community.

Acknowledgments

We are deeply indebted to countless individuals who have trained, coached, and advised us throughout the years, making each of us a better educator and a better leader than we would have been otherwise. We offer all of them—educators, scientists, authors, practitioners, theorists, veterans, novices, students, friends, and family—our deepest thanks. Their professionalism, dedication, commitment, and friendship shaped us and, therefore, helped shape this book.

Corwin Press would like to thank the following individuals for their contributions to the work:

Donna Adkins
Teacher
Arkadelphia Public Schools
Arkadelphia, AR

Amy Allen
Educational Consultant
Baton Rouge, LA

Jane Belmore, PhD
Edgewood College
Educational Leadership
  Doctoral Faculty
Madison, WI

Gustava Cooper-Baker
Principal
Sanford B. Ladd African
  Centered School
Kansas City, MO

Elizabeth F. Day
Grade 6 Teacher
2005 New York State
  Teacher of the Year
Mechanicville Middle School
Mechanicville, NY

Roberta E. Glaser, Ph.D.
Assistant Superintendent,
  Retired
St. Johns Public Schools
St. Johns, MI

Joen Hendricks-Painter
Educational Consultant
Independent Contractor
Yuma, AZ

Renee Peoples
Teacher
Swain West
Bryson City, NC

Stephen D. Shepperd
Principal
Sunnyside Elementary
  School
Kellogg, ID

About the Authors

Photograph by Barbara J. Klimek, 2007

Karl J. Klimek is the Executive Orchestrator of the Convergence Education Foundation, a nonprofit organization that incorporates brain/mind learning theory and practices in schools, with special focus on science, engineering, and mathematics projects (www.cef-trek.org). He is coauthor of *12 Brain-Mind Learning Principles in Action: The Fieldbook for Making Connections, Teaching, and the Human Brain* (2004, Corwin Press) and has taught in Washington, Wyoming, and Michigan at both the public school and university levels. His school administrative experience includes service as a principal and as assistant superintendent for curriculum and instruction in a suburban Detroit district. Karl is President of 2 Perspectives: Learning Through Leadership (www.2perspectives.org) and has worked extensively in career and technology education developing state and federal programs. Karl received his undergraduate degree in education from Central Washington

University and his master's in educational leadership from Eastern Michigan University. He is recognized for his practical and enthusiastic presentations as a speaker and workshop facilitator and is a private pilot.

Elsie Ritzenhein (Far Right, Author Photo) is the Director of the Macomb Academy of Arts and Sciences in Armada, Michigan, a magnet school for mathematics, science, and technology designed around a foundation of generativity, living systems, and brain/mind learning research. She is also President and CEO of Creative Sources, where she uses her vast experience as a principal, teacher, central office administrator, Title I director, arts administrator, and school board member to assist educators and leaders in designing and implementing generative environments in schools. She has consulted for many years in K–12 areas such as language arts, the fine and performing arts, creativity, integrated curriculum and instruction, and brain/mind teaching and learning as well as working with community college faculty. Elsie has held adjunct faculty positions at a number of colleges and universities in Michigan, most recently Saginaw Valley State University. She is also currently on the faculty of the Natural Learning Research Institute (http://naturallearninginstitute.org) and is a Senior Associate with Caine Learning (www.cainelearning.com). She lives in Shelby Township, Michigan, with her two cats, Pearl and Lena, and near her son Rob and her daughter-in-law Nicole. Elsie is passionate about creating school and organizational environments in which all stakeholders and participants can work toward their full learning and creative potential.

Dr. Kathryn D. Sullivan (Far Left, Author Photo) is a scientist, astronaut, and award-winning educator. She currently serves as the founding Director of the Battelle Center for Mathematics & Science Education Policy in the John Glenn School of Public Affairs at the Ohio State University (www.glennschool.osu.edu). During her 15 years with NASA, she flew on three space shuttle missions and earned the distinction of being the first American woman to walk in space. She served as Chief Scientist of the National Oceanic and Atmospheric Administration (NOAA) from 1993 to 1996. Moving to Columbus, Ohio, in 1996, she became President and CEO of COSI (Ohio's Center of Science & Industry), one of the nation's premiere centers for hands-on science and public outreach. Recognizing her lifelong work in science education, the National Science Board awarded her its Public Service Medal in 2003. Soon after, she was appointed to that board by the President of the United States, and now serves as Vice Chairman. Kathy is an acclaimed speaker on the national and international levels and a strong advocate for bringing the passion and creativity of real science into the heart of teaching and learning.

Please visit our Generative Leadership Web site: www.generative-educator.com

We dedicate this book to all those who are committed to shaping a new future for our schools—the future our children so richly deserve.

Prologue

Imagine the day when every child approaches the entrance of your school eager to begin the exciting, purposeful day he or she knows is in store. Imagine the day when your entire staff—professional and nonprofessional alike—melds their responsibilities, goals, and skills together seamlessly, creating a safe learning environment that engages each learner effectively in a challenging, varied, and experience-based curriculum. Imagine the atmosphere of a school in which everybody shares the latest research on learning and sees new knowledge as a compass that guides the continual improvement of the teaching and learning environment. Imagine your own school being like this! Imagine the benefit for our children of developing in such a vibrant learning environment!

Sadly, too few of today's schools fit this description. Administrators and teachers alike wrestle with time and budget pressures, complex regulations and procedures, external mandates, constraints on instructional content and methods, and huge administrative reporting burdens. This struggling state of American schools is decried by countless critics and stakeholders, each of whom offers a different preferred prescription for systemic improvement. The external forces shaping American society today—demographic change, economic insecurity, the speed of our digital world, and popular culture's celebration of personality, wealth, and excess—shape our schools as well, affecting both their internal cultures and their relationships with their community. Instead of "civic dialogue" on societal challenges we have "talk" shows that are little more than shouting matches and media designed to make sure we never consider differing viewpoints thoughtfully. In such a climate, with such pressures, how is it possible to solve tough problems or even to make progress on them? How do we get the complex problems we face "unstuck"?

Schools are not the only organizations that struggle with pressures, constraints, and complex social interactions. Realizing this, we turned to the worlds of business, governance, and social change for insight. Our thesis was not that schools should be more like corporations or that a technique from the world of business or government could be simply replicated in schools. Instead, we wondered whether the organizational change research and practice in these settings revealed principles that might also apply to schools. Through many years of research, study with leading practitioners, and practical work testing key concepts in school settings, we concluded that there is, indeed, something for school leaders to learn from these other domains: generative leadership.

Generative leadership is an approach to leading within organizations—any organization, from your family to your school or a large corporation—that recognizes and taps the collective intelligence and energy within an organization to generate productive growth and effective solutions. We see generative leadership as a

> How do we get the complex problems we face "unstuck"?

fusion of three foundational elements: generativity, living systems principles, and brain/mind science. In practice, these foundational elements are woven together inseparably, but in a book, they have to be covered sequentially. Thus, the first three chapters of this volume give a brief summary of each foundational element in turn, tracing their roots in the social and physical sciences and highlighting the insights most relevant for school leaders. Recaps of key points and questions for reflection are included at the ends of chapters. Reflection, an essential step in the brain's natural learning process, is often left out of schooling and training. Your time with this book will be more effective if you take some time for this practice. The questions offered will help you synthesize the new information and begin to relate it to your prior experience and your own school.

> By design, this is a brief, nontechnical book.

The real purpose of this book is to help school leaders bring these elements to life in their classrooms and conference rooms. This is the central focus of the last three chapters. Chapter 4 begins by looking at how the three foundational elements fuse together into generative school leadership. It opens with a look at generative learning environments that includes links to brain/mind principles and current leadership strategies. The focus then shifts to leadership and the leader, identifying four modalities that generative leaders have in their repertoire and six hallmarks that can guide the development of an individual's generative capacity. Finally, we offer 10 operational indicators that school leaders can use to assess both their individual progress and their school organization.

The final two chapters are all about practice. Chapter 5 provides an overview of several social technologies that we have found effective in our own work. These range from simple tools anyone can apply immediately in his or her own school to more complex processes designed to help multi-stakeholder groups tackle tough problems and envision new futures. The "catalysts for growth" in Chapter 6 are tools for personal growth and organizational development. Use them to guide assessments, prompt individual and group reflection, or start a conversation within your school. We have learned never to be proud about our generative capacity or leadership skills—there is always more to learn and room to grow. We offer these catalysts in that spirit.

By design, this is a brief, nontechnical book. The literature on leadership and on each of the foundational topics we cover is immense, however, which made our task quite daunting. The final product, inevitably, will be judged too simplistic by some and too dense or arcane by others. We can only say that we strived mightily to craft a sound balance between competing properties such as length and depth, readability and academic precision. We appreciate the many reviewers who helped us with this challenge and accept final responsibility for any shortcomings.

In closing, some words of caution. A leader's work is challenging, complex, and dynamic, and generative leadership defies reduction to a simple how-to formula. Furthermore, as educators and leaders, we know that something invented or learned by someone in one setting cannot be transplanted mechanically, in cut-and-paste fashion, into another setting. So you'll find no simple checklists, standard templates, or quick fixes here. We offer instead seeds of understanding that you can nurture through your own reflection, active practice, and continual learning. This is hard work, but these seeds will yield rich fruit for your school, your students, and you as a school leader.

Generativity 1

The First Foundational Element

I don't know how you do it, nor why sometimes. But because you do, it makes a difference in what I do.

This has been one of the busiest weeks I have had since starting here three years ago. I wasn't exactly the model of "eager teacher" arriving first in the a.m., but I stayed late three days and went on to something school-related at 7:00 every evening.

I was telling C. yesterday that the week was catching up to me; how I was ready to just do nothing over the break. Then I started joking with him that we've done quite a lot. We ought to just sit back for a year and rest and start working hard again next year.

Three years ago that would have been easy. Then you had to come here. Your example is quietly powerful. I am aware of how many things you are involved with and all of the things you do around here. You don't dictate. You just lead. It is the greatest management style I have been exposed to.

It is a little gift that you give to me, daily. So Merry Christmas to me, from you. All I can try to do is mimic it to a fraction of a degree. I won't succeed in emulating it 100 percent, but I'll try.

—Holiday note from a teacher to a principal, 2003

W hat if this note had been in your mailbox? Wouldn't it have made your day? What kind of leadership moved one of your teachers to write so warmly about "your quiet example" and to be so grateful that "you just lead"?

We see in this letter vivid testimony to some of the essential qualities of a generative leader. This is a principal who taps and guides the creative energies of the entire school team. Her bearing and actions as a leader have fostered an environment of appreciation, respect, and personal reflection in the entire school. This leader recognizes that everybody in the school is being shaped in new ways by every experience, from the students learning in a classroom to the teachers and staff coming together to develop new curriculum or plan professional development. This awareness permeates every aspect of how she leads.

WHY GENERATIVE LEADERSHIP?

What are the benefits of this kind of leadership, specifically for our schools? This short holiday note highlights a very important one: the positive effects for everyone of working in a constructive and supportive management environment. This principal's example, her very way of being, draws forth commitment and energy from the staff and sustains them through their tough or tired periods.

> Generative leaders are intent on bringing to light new possibilities for action and growth.

There are other benefits as well. Generative leaders are intent on bringing to light new possibilities for action and growth. They bring to their work a powerful blend of knowledge, personal mastery, high energy, creative thinking, and willingness to take action. These individual qualities, plus the skill at tapping the intelligence and creativity that resides in everybody around them, combine to allow generative leaders to fulfill this intention for their schools.

This principal has the responsibilities and authority typical of any principal and faces the same deliverables and array of challenges. The way she enacts them is usually quite different from that of a stereotypical authoritarian leader. More often than not, her approach is one of guiding rather than giving orders or directions. Her aim is to release the initiative of her staff and students rather than to dictate their actions or

Generative leadership will give school leaders powerful new understanding of the dynamic systems they are guiding and help them tackle more effectively the complex challenges of their environment.

control their time. They collaborate with her in setting goals and objectives and defining their approach to realizing them. The principal is open to allowing their individual knowledge and creativity to govern the final product. In other words, she allows control of the final details to reside with the team and to emerge from its collective work.

This is not to say that this principal handles every problem or decision she faces in a generative fashion. Her experience as a leader gives her sound judgment about which circumstances she should direct, in the fashion typical of command-and-control leadership modalities, and which ones she can guide in a generative fashion. For skilled leaders, this is not an "either-or" choice but a "both-and" option.

Leading in this way is sometimes likened to an improvisational dance: The starting point on the dance floor is clear, but how the dance will go and where it will end up depend completely on what the musician plays and how the dancer responds to that music. With true improvisation, neither the musician nor the dancer is in command. Neither has planned his or her actions in advance, and the precise outcome cannot be predicted ahead of time. Musician and dancer co-create the performance in real time, guided by shared knowledge, values, and intention.

Many of the problems facing today's school leaders will clearly not yield to repetitive and more intensive command-and-control efforts. Generative leadership will give school leaders powerful new understanding of the dynamic systems they are guiding and help them tackle more effectively the complex challenges of their environment. A good place to begin building an understanding of generative leadership is with the concept of generativity itself. The context from which generativity emerged is also important to this understanding, and, for that, we need to make a brief detour into history.

LIKE CLOCKWORK

The dominant framework of our culture is one of machines, one in which we function as engineers, diagnosing what's wrong with a machine and fixing the part that isn't working right. "What is that pinging noise? What parts do I need to oil, replace, or repair?" Engineering problems can be solved through careful observations of the physical system and logical, analytical reasoning that links the symptom we observe to one or more individual parts or components. Whether the problem involves a car engine, an air conditioner, or a spacecraft, it can be understood in this way—by breaking it down into its separate parts. The same model is reflected clearly in our approach to organizations. When an organization is not performing as desired, we look for flaws in its parts (the unit or division, function or process) and consider how to "fix" it (by *reengineering*, *aligning*, or *reconfiguring* the parts). Is this vocabulary common in your school or district?

This vocabulary of machines and engineering reflects the conceptual model that has dominated our society's collective thinking and actions for centuries. The roots of this influence go back to the philosopher–scientists of the 17th century, especially to Sir Isaac Newton. His famous *Principia*, written in 1687, described a wonderful and orderly universe, made up of objects whose actions followed simple laws, rather like the mechanism of a grand mechanical clock. Newton's physics gave people a powerful, predictive understanding of the world around them. For the first time, it seemed possible that mere mortals might be able to understand the workings of the universe and control their physical environment.

Though Newton warned against making too much of the machinelike orderliness of his universe, the clockwork image was irresistibly simple and powerful. Over the next three centuries, it permeated Western science and culture, becoming the predominant metaphor or mental model by which we make sense of, talk about, and relate to both our physical and our social worlds. It shapes some of Western society's most deeply embedded expectations of reality, and these expectations determine how our society engages with the world. As organizational development expert and author Meg Wheatley (1992) puts it, "For three centuries we've been planning, predicting and analyzing the world . . . we grew assured of the role of determinism and prediction. We absorbed expectations of regularity into our very beings. And we organized work and knowledge based on our beliefs about this predictable universe" (p. 26).

Unfortunately, many countries and cultures are employing a late twentieth-century political process in an attempt to perfect an early twentieth-century model of schools, based on seventeenth-century beliefs about how people learn, in order to prepare children for the twenty-first century. (Caine & Caine, 2001, p. iv)

Our schools were organized based on this universe, too. Today's schools, designed to meet societal and labor needs of more than a century ago, borrowed directly from the machine-based organization model of factories. This heritage is clear in the hierarchical structure of authority, the division of knowledge into small units, and the dividing of the day into manageable blocks of time. Content strands, standards and benchmarks, Carnegie units and class schedules all reflect our desire for orderliness and the Newtonian presumptions of regularity and predictability in the universe.

ATOMS AND ORGANIZATIONS

Newton's elegant model of an orderly, clockwork universe dominated scientific inquiry until the early 20th century. When scientists began to study the atom, however, it soon became clear that Sir Isaac's laws were not universal after all. The motions observed inside the nucleus of the atom did not obey Newton's laws of motion, which were hypothesized to be true everywhere and for all things. Other research turned up further problems. For example, physicists discovered that light behaved both like a wave and like a particle, and that it's not possible to know both the precise position and the velocity of an electron: Only a probability of these can be measured. A new theory called quantum mechanics soon emerged to account for these non-Newtonian phenomena. The very names of some of quantum theory's cornerstones—"Heisenberg's uncertainty principle" and the "wave-particle duality," for example—suggest how utterly different this new world of randomness and probability is from Sir Isaac's neatly ordered clockwork universe.

> A new theory called quantum mechanics soon emerged to account for these non-Newtonian phenomena.

As it went with atoms, so it soon came to be with organizations. Starting in the 1950s and accelerating in the late 1980s, theorists and consultants began to think there had to be a better way to tackle the tough and increasingly complex problems faced by human organizations. They probed deeply into just how the Newtonian model affected the behaviors and decisions of organizations and turned to fields such as systems dynamics, quantum mechanics, and complexity theory for new insight. Generativity is one of the important new concepts that came from this work. Let's look more closely at some of the key events in its emergence and trace how it eventually began to transform ideas about leadership.

SOCIAL SCIENCE ROOTS

Psychologist Ken Gergen was one of the first people to use the word *generative* in print (Gergen, 1978), in a paper about social science theory. Gergen felt that most social science theory lacked "generative potency," meaning "the capacity to challenge prevailing assumptions . . . and to offer fresh alternatives to contemporary patterns of conduct" (p. 1344).

> Gergen felt the field of social sciences would stagnate intellectually . . .

The reason for this, he believed, was that most social scientists had come to accept one overarching worldview—he called it a "meta-theory"—so deeply that the fundamental assumptions it rested on were no longer questioned or tested. The most critical of these presumptions were empiricism and reductionism: the ideas that only observable, material phenomena were meaningful and that complex behaviors can be understood by understanding in detail the smaller building blocks of which they were made. As a result, most of the research in the field consisted of amassing greater quantities of data, improving measurement precision, or searching for the organizing principles or computer methods that might transform the vast volumes of data into meaningful knowledge. Any proposed experiment that didn't fit this mold would be rejected rather than celebrated as potentially transformative.

This bothered Gergen because of something the history of his field revealed. The important, innovative ideas of social science in the prior century had not come about from ever-more precise analysis of what was already accepted as "known." Instead, they were departures from the "common-sense assumptions" of the day. They were generative theories that threw the commonly shared assumptions into question, fostering sharp debate, incisive inquiry and conversation across the lines of academic disciplines. Ultimately, profound new understandings of the social world and new options for action emerged from this ferment. Gergen felt the field of social sciences would stagnate intellectually and lose its relevance to society without the creativity and new learning that generative theory could provide.

AN APPRECIATIVE EYE

This concept of generative theory had a profound influence on a young doctoral student at Ohio's Case Western Reserve University in the mid-1980s (Watkins & Mohr, 2001). David Cooperrider was working on an organizational analysis of the Cleveland Clinic, a premier medical facility in Ohio. His assignment was to find out what was wrong with the human side of the organization. Setting out on a series of staff interviews to gather the data for this analysis he was surprised to find that a tremendous amount of positive cooperation, egalitarianism, and innovation existed within the clinic. Then he came across Gergen's work on generative theory. This pointed him toward an entirely new way of thinking about the clinic and his task.

Cooperrider saw in Gergen's generative theory an "anticipatory theory that has the capacity to challenge the guiding assumptions of the culture, to raise fundamental questions regarding contemporary life, to foster reconsideration of that which is taken for granted, and thereby furnish new alternatives for social action" (Watkins & Mohr, 2001, p. 16). Armed with this insight, and having secured his advisor's blessing, he persuaded the clinic's chairman to change the project from an assessment of what was *wrong* to a study of what was *right*, an assessment of the positive factors that contributed to the clinic's highly effective functioning.

This approach led Cooperrider to formulate a new strategy for organizational change known as appreciative inquiry

(Cooperrider & Srivastava, 1987). Chapter 5 provides more information on the principles and methods of appreciative inquiry. For now, it's enough to note its central argument, which is that deficit-based or problem-solving approaches to organizational development are not sufficient to the complex challenges confronting modern leaders.

Generative approaches

- Challenge commonsense assumptions
- Raise fundamental questions
- Foster reconsideration of that which is taken for granted
- Furnish new alternatives for action and new prospects for the future

---

LESSONS FROM SCIENCE

Cooperrider was neither the first nor the only researcher to find powerful insights about organizations in fields outside business and management. Meg Wheatley (1992), quoted previously, studied advances in the physical sciences, looking for new insights to give managers and leaders. She describes her learning journey through fields such as quantum physics, biology and ecology, complexity and chaos in *Leadership and the New Science,* one of the seminal books of this time.

Peter Senge, an engineer at the Massachusetts Institute of Technology, is another noteworthy researcher in this arena. Senge was part of a group that had been applying engineering insights to the study of organizations since the late 1950s. His research with corporations showed that the machine-oriented vocabulary used by people in many companies reflects a deeply rooted mental model that drives the behavior and actions of workers and leaders alike. In this model, the organization is a structure. When something is wrong (with the company's products or employee turnover or profits), the solution is believed implicitly to lie in fixing the structure. In companies guided by these mental models, Senge also found that the primary approach to solving problems was reductionist, based on the presumption that solutions to complex problems could always be found by breaking them down into simpler elements that one could understand in great detail. The leaders and managers Senge worked with considered the ideas of organization-as-structure and reductionism to be factual, commonsense statements about reality and so never questioned them deeply. Senge, however, recognized that they were really just widely shared assumptions that were engrained deeply within the organization (Senge, 1990).

Senge, Wheatley, and Cooperrider all recognized that organizations were increasingly facing challenges more complex than the company's existing mental models (more on these in Chapter 2) and management methods could handle. Some of these challenges were external, perhaps in the form of new competitors or accelerating business cycles, while others came from the increasing complexity of the company itself. This new class of challenges often had many factors changing simultaneously and involved complex interactions with stakeholders across the company and in the outside world. It was not possible for any single person anywhere within the organizational structure to know all the information relevant to an effective solution or to be aware of all the interactions that would make a solution either fail or succeed in implementation. Many companies struggled in the face of such challenges, and some failed. Others, however, managed to solve the tough, complex problems they faced and overcome the challenges. In simple terms, both Senge and Wheatley concluded that companies holding rigidly to mechanistic mental models and rigid leadership modes were the ones that stumbled or failed. Companies that were able to question their most deeply held assumptions and find ways to tap the knowledge and creativity of all their associates were the ones that survived and thrived.

The nature of the company's leadership was the key factor determining which path they took. Leaders in the flexible, resilient, successful companies did not see their organization as a structure or as a set of boxes and lines on an organizational chart. Instead, they saw it as a web

> These leaders saw that they were responding to and living in a dynamic ecosystem, not a mechanical structure.

of interconnections and interdependencies linking myriad nodes of energy (expertise and information) inside the company and interacting continually with the world around it. Leading with this view is very different from attempting to control a machine. These leaders saw that they were responding to and living in a dynamic ecosystem, not a mechanical structure. Their role was not to control the assignments of time and energy to elements of activity, as in the outworn industrial model. It was, instead, to release and guide the initiative, talent, and energy within their organization. This alone could create the solutions and new possibilities the company would need to overcome the challenges of the day and have the resilience needed to respond to the utterly unpredictable challenges of the future.

DEFINING GENERATIVITY

Generativity is what let the company leaders that Senge and Wheatley studied get their companies "unstuck" when they came up against the tough problems of their times. The leadership of these successful companies moved beyond the reductionist, hierarchical patterns of the past. As they fostered generativity throughout the organization, they found that finding solutions was no longer the exclusive domain of formal leaders, nor was merely following instructions from on high the role of associates. Instead, new approaches were co-created and carried out by many people throughout the system. Generative learning is the type of organizational learning that emphasizes systemic thinking, a willingness to question the supposed limits of an issue, to think creatively outside the assumed constraints and continuous experimentation (Cooperrider, Whitney, & Stavros, 2003).

If you do an Internet search, you'll find the words *generativity* and *generative* cropping up in a variety of circles, with different meanings in each one. For example, in the elder care arena, "generative care" describes an approach grounded in a strong sense of moral obligation that unites generations. In social and cognitive sciences, it connotes the generating of shared meaning within a group of people.

The essential meaning of generativity as we use it in this book closely follows the dictionary definition of the word *generative:*

Generativity is the capacity or ability to create, produce, or give rise to new constructs, new possibilities.

The challenges confronting school leaders today have much in common with those faced by the companies studied by Wheatley, Senge, and others: many stakeholders, competing priorities, scarce resources, external scrutiny, complex regulations, high expectations, and high stakes. Our experiences as leader–educators taught us that these common points outweigh the differences when it comes to judging whether the insights gained from the business sphere can be adapted for application to our schools. Unfortunately, it seems that few school leaders realize this or apply this thinking to their daily efforts. Like the struggling leaders Senge studied, most school leaders under high stress resort to comfortable and known methods, too often settling for doing just what's needed to survive each day as successfully as possible. Focusing on creativity and collaborating to generate new possibilities seems impossible under such duress.

Generative leadership is not just another management device or vocabulary set for leaders to add to their toolkit, however. It involves a fundamental shift in the mental models by which leaders and their followers perceive, respond to, and interact with the world around them, both the world inside their school and the external environment. In a real sense, then, generative leadership becomes a way of being rather than just a new set of techniques for doing the work of the leader. Some key traits of generative leaders are easily observed in words and actions:

- They see their school as a dynamic system and every individual as an integral element of that system, affecting its present behavior and future conditions.
- Their leadership is more collaborative than authoritarian and is intent on realizing the potential and possibilities inherent in their students, their staff, and the entire school.
- They recognize the pervasive influence of individual and collective mental models and constantly question the assumptions embedded in them.
- They see the future as very shapeable but neither precisely predictable nor controllable to the last detail.
- A focus on initiative, ideas, and innovation dominates their working style, with strong directive action reserved for moments that truly require it.
- A constructive spirit of collaboration in envisioning and achieving an outstanding future is genuinely present in every interaction, from meetings and presentations to individual encounters.

Today's school leaders must meet great demands and tackle complex challenges. We emphasize again that the old machine- or factory-based model of managing will not provide them with the full range of insights needed to meet these challenges and lead their schools effectively in difficult times. Generative leadership—leadership that understands the organization as a dynamic system possessing much more capacity than mechanistic mental models recognize—brings forward important new perspectives and capacities for school leaders. It gives them a new way to understand and engage with the complex environment within and around their school. It doesn't dilute their authority, nor does it rule out directives or eliminate the management of projects by tasks and assignments. Think of it as a multiplier, drawing out the combined insight, creativity, and capacity of everyone in the school and enabling everybody to continue thinking and acting constructively even without the leader's presence or direction. Most important, generative leadership furnishes new alternatives for action and so offers new prospects for our schools.

RECAP

Shared assumptions govern a group's choices, behaviors, and sense of what is possible. These shared assumptions are usually invisible and unspoken, so they escape questioning and testing.

The machine-like Newtonian mental model prevalent in Western society has a strong effect on how we view organizations and tackle the problems confronting us.

Generativity is the capacity or ability to create, produce, or give rise to new constructs, new possibilities.

GENERATIVE LEADERSHIP

- Challenges the commonsense assumptions

- Raises fundamental questions

- Fosters reconsideration of that which is taken for granted

- Thinks creatively outside the supposed limits of a problem to identify new alternatives for action and new prospects for the future.

REFLECTIONS

- How are problems talked about in your school? What evidence do you have that machine-like metaphors are common? Do they affect the range of actions considered?

- Can you identify one or two of the shared assumptions in your school that are commonly taken as absolute fact but that might be worth testing? How would you test these?

- What blend of authoritarian and collaborative leadership is common in your school? How much does the blend you observe depend on circumstances and how much on the individual approach of specific leaders?

- When have you been vividly aware of the dynamic interactions that link a group of individuals into a system? How did you feel? What circumstances brought this about?

- What possible futures do you see for your school and/or district? How might you begin to think in a generative way about designing and implementing those futures?

- What is working for you as a leader? For your school? How can you generate more of what is working? Who needs to participate in that conversation?

Living Systems

2

The Second Foundational Element

We must conceive of living systems as systems of elements in mutual dynamic interaction, and discover the laws that govern the pattern of parts and processes.

—Ludwig Von Bertalanffy (in Kamaryt, 1973, p. 77)

The second foundational element of generative leadership is the understanding that organizations as different as companies, cities, and schools are best understood as dynamic systems rather than just collections of parts. The word *system* means an integral working combination of elements forming a complex or unitary whole and hints at the paramount importance of the interactions among all the elements. The word *dynamic* means that the system and all its elements are constantly changing, adapting, and evolving. When we shift from a Newtonian view to a systems view, the focus changes from parts to the organization of parts, from component and role to interconnections and dynamics.

EARLY DEVELOPMENTS

Like the concept of generativity, the focus on the dynamics of systems and the properties emerging from these was born first in philosophy and the natural sciences and later applied to organizations. The roots of system theory can be traced back to the 17th-century philosophers such as Leibniz, but its blossoming began in the middle of the 20th century. The evolution of systems theory into systems science as we know it today came about through the work of many scientists, working in fields as diverse as anthropology, physics, biology, and engineering.

It's worth noting that these founding scientists all worked without modern tools. Their only tools were pencil, paper, and in some cases, mathematics. They achieved profound understanding of complex systems through careful observation, deep reflection, the formulation of new concepts, and the testing of these against further observations.

> Imagine thinking that every single car had to be learned individually . . .

Hungarian biologist Ludwig von Bertalanffy (1968) provided a solid foundation for systems science with his *General Systems Theory*. The aim of this work was to describe the universal "models, principles, and laws" that apply to all types and classes of systems, not just to one specific system or another. One way to appreciate the power of such a unifying theory is to consider a simple parallel with everyday life. Imagine thinking that every single car had to be learned individually, because nobody had recognized there were principles (of design, of operation, of maintenance) that all cars had in common! With these stated clearly, researchers in many fields could examine all kinds of systems and test how well they applied.

Psychologist James Grier Miller was interested in a particular class of systems—living systems. Like Bertalanffy, he sought to develop a unified theory that described how all living systems work, how they maintain themselves, develop, and change (Miller, 1978; Miller & Miller, 1997). Miller's theory identifies eight levels of living systems, starting at the cell and increasing in complexity. The higher-complexity levels in this spectrum include organizations, communities, nations, and supranational bodies (such as the European Union or International Monetary Fund). According to Miller's theory, every system in each of these eight levels has in common 20 subsystems. These process the exchanges of information, matter, and energy that are essential to life and survival.

ENTER THE ENGINEERS

Mathematics and engineering provided other important strands to systems theory, along with powerful new tools (Forrester, 1989; the following adapted from this source). The great surge in science and engineering mounted to win World War II produced a number of these. One of the central challenges of the war was to control complex systems amid the ever-changing conditions of battle. The Massachusetts Institute of Technology (MIT) was home to a key laboratory that was working to solve this problem, and one of this group's vital tasks was to figure out how to automatically aim and fire antiaircraft guns.

Many of the great pioneers of feedback control systems, computing, and systems modeling were in this group. Together, they developed the mathematical equations, computers, and control mechanisms needed by the U.S. Army and Navy. They constantly received field performance data from the front lines so that they could improve their models and send back new equations for the computers before the next enemy attack—talk about high-stakes testing!

Most of the scientists and engineers from this group went on to become pioneers in computers, cognitive research, and artificial intelligence, but a few took a different route. They decided after the war to explore whether the engineering insights they had gained could help corporations solve their own complex, dynamic problems. The Sloan School of Management was established at MIT specifically to bring the focus and methods of engineering to the problems of companies and other organizations. Starting in the late 1950s, the Sloan group's work began to produce important new insights about how a scientific understanding of complex, dynamic systems can help people in companies, civic organizations, and education.

Jay Forrester was one of the engineers who shifted over to the Sloan School. A young engineer during the war years, he had become expert in feedback control systems and in methods for modeling their dynamic behavior. To build such models, he had to first identify every element and all the interactions within a system. Then he had to translate this logical map into the mathematical expressions of computing. These models had worked very well on the very tough wartime problems, but could they actually apply to organizations? Would they really give leaders a better understanding of why different internal policies produced success or failure? Forrester set off to find out, focusing first on the business cycles experienced by computer companies.

FEEDBACK: THE MISSING LOOPS

It became apparent very quickly that systems dynamic modeling did indeed provide leaders with powerful new understanding of their company's behavior. The models revealed many previously unrecognized links between corporate policies and decisions and business outcomes. One insight in particular usually came as a big surprise to leaders: the critical ways in which an organization's mental models affect how it behaves and how it responds to both challenges and opportunities. Trained to focus on administrative structure and business processes, banishing human factors from consideration, most of the leaders Forrester worked with were unaware of the pervasive influence exerted by these models and shocked at their impact on company performance.

We all use mental models to simplify and make sense of the world around us. They literally affect how we "see" a situation, and they play a powerful role in how we decide to respond. Filters and lenses are familiar metaphors that can help us understand this influence more clearly. Our mental models are the lenses through which we perceive each and every experience; there is no pathway to our consciousness that bypasses them. They also act as filters, helping us sort and categorize new inputs very quickly and align them with what is already familiar. Modern neuroscience research reveals that mental models have a physiological basis. They reflect the neuronal patterns in our brain that prior experiences have forged. Chapter 3 provides a fuller overview of recent research into the brain/mind

> Mental models are formed by our past experiences and reflect our existing knowledge.

system and the rich linkages between biology and cognition it reveals. For now, it's enough to understand that people interact with the world around them via mental models. They are intrinsic mechanisms in human cognition.

Mental models are formed by our past experiences and reflect our existing knowledge. They are typically very simplistic representations of much more complex phenomena and events. Every person in an organization, whether it's a business or a school, brings a uniquely individual set of mental models to each event and interaction. These are always active but, typically, beyond our awareness. They're embedded so deeply in our consciousness that they seem to be reality and so escape critical examination, just like the assumptions that Gergen recognized were embedded deeply in the accepted theoretical framework of social theory in his time.

One key benefit of Forrester's systems modeling approach is that it forces the people in a school or company to capture all the elements and interactions in their system well enough to make a computer simulation. This process forces the assumptions that underlie both individual and collective mental models into the open, where they can be challenged and tested. The computer models and the mental models are not opposing methods but, rather, as Forrester (1996) puts it, "overlapping and mutually reinforcing ways to understand reality" (p. 22).

COMPLEX SYSTEMS, SIMPLE MODELS

Working over the years with many companies, large urban cities and educational systems, Forrester came to understand why our intuitive mental models so often produce bad results in organizations: They are far too simple to help us anticipate the real behavior of complex systems. The problem is not with the mental models we construct of various *parts* of a system—such as who reports to whom, who has what information, or what a given unit is trying to achieve. These are usually rich enough to help us understand the parts separately. But a system is not just a heap of parts. It's a unitary entity in which all the parts interact through a complex web of relationships and

> A system is not just a heap of parts.

exchanges. Our simple intuitive mental models typically omit complex interactions and feedback loops, so they cannot possibly guide us to envision or predict correctly how a complex system will behave.

> *Complex systems behave in ways entirely different from our expectations derived from experience with simple systems. Because intuition is based on simple systems, people are misled when making decisions about complex systems. . . .*

> *. . . Learning ever since childhood teaches lessons that cause people to misjudge and mismanage complex systems.* (Forrester, 1996, p. 10)

Peter Senge, whom we met in Chapter 1, is one of Forrester's protégés. His best-selling book *The Fifth Discipline* (Senge, 1990) synthesized the system dynamics group's key findings along with his own research on many successful companies. Senge made a powerful argument that systems dynamics should become an essential discipline for leaders, helping them confront more effectively the complex and dynamic challenges of our modern society. *The Fifth Discipline* also made the principles of systems dynamics accessible to the general public and broadened tremendously its circle of practitioners and devotees. Senge and Forrester remain active in research and consulting practice. Education is now one main thrust of their work, as they try to bring systems dynamics modeling into the classroom (Senge, Cambron McCabe, Lucas, & Kleiner, 2000).

LESSONS FROM NATURE

Meg Wheatley is another organizational development expert who felt that the common organization-as-machine model was no longer sufficient and began to search for a new conceptual framework to replace it. Wheatley undertook an intensive study of the latest advances in the physical sciences, in the rapidly growing field of systems science, and in emerging fields such as chaos theory and complexity. Melding these together with her organizational work, Wheatley's *Leadership and the New Science* (1992) proposed a new approach to leadership, one that emphasizes the dynamics of an organization rather than its structure—a living systems approach to leading organizations.

Why would it matter whether leaders think of their organizations as structures or as living systems? Today's organizations, our schools included, exist in a world of continual change. To survive—not to mention remain effective—it's essential that they continually evolve, adapt, and revitalize themselves. Machines cannot do these things. Machines execute the functions built or programmed into them to accomplish a specified set of desired tasks. They function successfully only in the operating conditions for which they were designed. So why, asks Wheatley (2005) in *Finding Our Way*, would anybody want an organization to be like a machine?

> *A self-organizing system is one that is literally a whole that is greater than the sum of its parts. It is defined as a system that is created from components that are in existence and that spontaneously reorganize themselves to create something new, without the influence of any external force or executive plan. Control over a self-organized system is not centralized. It is distributed over the entire system.* (Andreasen, 2005, p. 62)

ATTRIBUTES OF LIVING SYSTEMS

By definition, living systems are adaptive, self-renewing, resilient, learning, and intelligent. They respond spontaneously, without central direction, to stresses and disturbances in ways that preserve essential functions and vitality. Wouldn't all leaders want their organizations to have this resiliency? It makes sense, then, for leaders to understand what properties of living systems give rise to these qualities and to work on bringing these to the fore in their organizations. The most salient properties of natural living systems are captured in the following points:

- Living systems are groups of simple individual entities linked by dense webs of interactions.

- Complexity and emergence are inherent features of living systems. Complexity is an essential richness rather than a troublesome messiness to be eliminated. Emergence means that the whole system has properties and capabilities that arise from the rich interactions of its components; the components themselves do not have all these properties or capabilities.

- Every individual within the system is constantly developing and, simultaneously, interacting with other parts of the system and with the environment outside the system. In other words, every element in the system co-participates with all the other elements in the evolutionary development of each individual. The combined action of all the elements co-creates the total system.

- The identity of each individual element is linked inextricably to and affected by the identity of the system, and vice versa. The system and its components co-develop and they co-create each other. In natural living systems, this occurs through exchanges of physical and chemical energy.

- Change is continuous for living systems. Indeed, it is an essential driver of growth, without which life ceases.

- The behavior of the whole system cannot be predicted based on an understanding of its individual parts, no matter how thoroughly each part is understood. It is the interactions among elements—the relationships or, in computer modeling vocabulary, the feedback loops, between them—that determine the system's properties and behaviors.

- Living systems are self-organizing. They respond spontaneously to disturbances, and the responses propagate throughout the entire system via the autonomous response of each individual element. In natural, open systems, these self-organizing responses always tend toward order and resiliency. The outwardly visible patterns one often sees in living systems are emergent, meaning they arise from the web of actions and interactions of the system rather than being imposed by a blueprint or an executive plan.

WHAT SCHOOL LEADERS CAN LEARN

School systems seem quite unlike organisms or ecosystems in almost every way imaginable. They are, after all, political structures designed well over a century ago on the basis of the mechanistic models passed down from Newton's time. Their boundaries are artificial geographical lines, and they typically function according to a very strict hierarchical model, like the 19th-century factories after which they were patterned.

Nonetheless, the principles of living systems can be seen in action at almost any school today. In the most authoritarian structure or harshest school culture, one may see only small sparks of it: a student who is curious about the gaps in what his teacher has said or one who struggles with class worksheets but shines in 4-H or scouting projects; the teacher who is immersed in a creative new initiative and whose contagious energy draws allies from across the school to her cause. These are small examples, to be sure, but each reflects some of the properties listed above and provides evidence that our schools can indeed function like living systems.

> *Self-organizing has been going on all the time, but our attention has been diverted to perfecting the controls and mechanisms that we thought were making work happen.* (Wheatley, 2005, p. 41)

What are the organizational equivalents of the natural living system properties listed above? Wheatley (2005, adapted below) shows that the essential conditions needed for organizations to self-organize and function like living systems fall into three domains: identity, information, and relationships.

Just like the foundational elements that make up generative leadership, these domains actually operate in a dynamic cycle and are so richly intertwined that the distinctions between them blur. Examining them separately at first will help school leaders identify the processes and structures they can focus on to bring the vitality, flexibility, and resiliency of living systems to their school.

Identity: The Sense-Making Capacity

An organization's identity includes more than just its mission, vision, and values. The current interpretations of its history, present decisions, and activities are also important. So is the organization's sense of its future. "Identity is both what we want to believe is true and what our actions show to be true about ourselves," notes Wheatley (2005, p. 38).

Information: The Medium

Information is data to which an organization has assigned meaning. In some organizations, it's seen as a commodity to be hoarded or traded for power and status. In living systems, information is an essential nutrient. It has to be freely flowing and present everywhere to sustain the system. When information is abundant and belongs to everyone, people can organize and adjust rapidly in response to shifting challenges and new opportunities.

Relationships: The Pathways

Information is created and transformed through relationships. People in an organization access its intelligence through the relationships—the sets of activities and exchanges—they have within the system. The organization expands its identity and becomes wiser through relationships with its external environment. The richer the connections are between people, the more possibilities there are. "In self-organizing systems, people need access to everyone; they need to be free to reach anywhere in the organization to accomplish work," Wheatley says (2005, p. 40).

Author Michael Fullan (2005) offers this idea: "If more and more leaders become systems thinkers, they will gravitate toward strategies that alter people's system-related experiences; that is, they will alter people's mental awareness of the system as a whole, thereby contributing to altering the system itself" (p. 40). Considering the interplay between identity, information, and relationships in your setting will yield deeper sensitivities to the interconnections that are sometimes visible and often invisible. Although not always apparent, these underlying threads contribute significantly to any leader's effectiveness.

RECAP

All humans engage the world around them through mental models that encode their prior experience. We are usually unaware of this processing and rarely examine these models critically.

Organizations have shared mental models that govern their choices and behaviors. Like an individual's mental models, these are rarely examined closely.

Both individuals and organizations deal with complex experiences and phenomena through extremely simplistic models of systems. These usually leave out many key elements and, perhaps more important, fail to include the feedback loops that give rise to the real system's properties and behavior.

Recognizing that organizations are systems rather than structures and thinking clearly about the elements and interactions (feedback loops) that compose them can make our mental models visible and help us improve upon them.

Living systems are adaptive, self-renewing, resilient, intelligent, and self-organizing. Understanding schools as living systems will help leaders better understand their dynamic, complexly networked properties.

Leaders can focus on three essential conditions to elicit and strengthen the living system properties of their school:

Identity—the sense-making capacity: The school's purpose and intent must be clear, shared, and genuine.

Information—the medium and essential nutrient of the school: It must be abundant and freely flowing.

Relationships—the pathways of the school: These must be authentic and richly networked throughout the organization.

REFLECTIONS

- What key traits are included in your mental model of the titled role you have at school? How are you participating in the changes that are happening over time within the system?

- Can you identify a collective mental model that shapes the behaviors and decisions of your school and the people within it? What does the model presume or take as an unchangeable fact?

- How clear a sense of identity does your school have? How do your students, teachers, and administrators share it? How do your students, teachers, and administrators express it? How does identity guide the central purpose of your school? How does it guide teaching and learning? How would you express your school's identity?

- Think about information as a commodity or a vital nutrient in your school. How is meaningful information sought and assimilated? How is this information used in a generative way? How does your staff self-organize around information that comes to them or that they seek?

- In what ways do you and your staff embrace a sense of being static and dynamic, of moving between control and emergence, of feeling isolated and connected? How do you create conversations and initiate actions that create a culture that supports "both/and"? (See Chapter 6 for a visual guide.)

- What are the important "pathways" in your school?

The
Brain/Mind
System

3

The Third Foundational Element

The main message is that learning is change. It is change in ourselves, because it is change in the brain. Thus the art of teaching must be the art of changing the brain. At least this much should be up front.

—James E. Zull (2002, p. xiv)

The human brain is perhaps the most marvelous example of a living system—a complex, adaptive system—in the universe. The three-pound organ sheltered by your skull contains hundreds of billions of neurons, each of which is capable of making tens of thousands of connections. This yields an astounding number of internal neuronal networks (i.e., groups of neurons that process in concert to perform various brain functions).

It was common in the 1960s and 1970s, even among neuroscientists, to think of the brain as a computer. Information-processing metaphors abounded, reflecting this widespread mental model. Particular brain regions or structures were seen as controlling or performing specific processes, just like each different module inside a computer performs its prescribed functions.

This mechanistic, hierarchical notion was overturned once modern technology let scientists observe the brains of healthy, awake animals that were responding to their entire environment. This type of study demonstrated clearly that the brain is a highly distributed, parallel processing system. Its many billion cells are connected through dense webs of neuronal pathways. It processes parts (such as specific stimuli or signals) and wholes (patterns, meanings, actions) at the same time and at multiple levels (from instinctual to conscious awareness). All its functions depend on and emerge from rich exchanges of signals and energy between the various regions conducted by these pathways. Some regions and pathways are more active than others in any given process, but most brain/mind functions involve multiple regions and processes acting in concert. In some cases, should one part of this amazing distributed processor be damaged or impaired by some stress, the system may respond by growing new cellular connections, and sometimes it makes new neuronal pathways, which at least partially restore the affected functions.

NATURAL LEARNING

How does the biology of the brain relate to human learning? This is the question that Dr. Jim Zull began to focus on in the mid-1990s. Zull is a biochemist whose research focused on cell-to-cell communication, protein-folding cell membranes, and biosensors. He also taught throughout his research career, earning many nominations for excellence along the way. In 1994, he was tapped to be the founding director of a new center for innovation in teaching and learning at Case Western Reserve University in Cleveland, Ohio. This assignment focused his attention squarely on how humans learn and on how science—especially neuroscience—might contribute to more effective teaching.

Immersing himself in cognitive science and educational research, he soon came across David Kolb's (1984) definitive work on experiential learning. Drawing heavily on the works of Dewey, Piaget, and others, Kolb had synthesized ideas on development and learning into a new "learning cycle." According to Kolb, deep learning—learning for real comprehension—occurs through a sequence of experience, reflection, abstraction, and active testing. In deep learning, we cycle through these stages repeatedly and concurrently, processing at multiple levels simultaneously.

> According to Kolb, deep learning—learning for real comprehension—occurs through a sequence of experience, reflection, abstraction, and active testing.

Zull (2002) describes his encounter with this model in *The Art of Changing the Brain*. He was skeptical at first. It is a very simple model, after all. Perhaps Kolb had managed to capture the vital essence of human learning, an amazingly rich process, in an elegantly simple form. But maybe his model was too simplistic to be instructive in any meaningful way. Zull found his answer before long, arriving at it through reasoning from biological principles. What he knew about the brain told him that Kolb's learning cycle should work, and it told him why:

> *In biology, the way things work depends on their structure— their physical structure. . . . Any function found in a living organism must depend on some structure of some part of that organism . . . and so it seemed that if the function we are interested in is learning, we should look for the structure that produces it, and the place we should look is in the brain. Ultimately, the structure of the brain should explain learning. It's only natural.* (Zull, 2002, p. 14)

Now seeing the brain as "a structure that evolved for human learning, for understanding and comprehension" (p. 14), Zull proceeded to define the correlation between brain structure and Kolb's four learning-cycle stages. He calls the result a model of natural learning.

HOW LEARNING CORRELATES TO STRUCTURE

One need not know how neurons and synapses work or remember the detailed anatomy of the brain to understand and work with this model. Four key processing regions of the cortex, or outer region of the brain, provide the needed linkage. The sensory cortex receives external sensory inputs. Two regions then integrate incoming data into higher-level information. The first of these, at the back of the brain, forms ideas and meaning

Figure 3.1

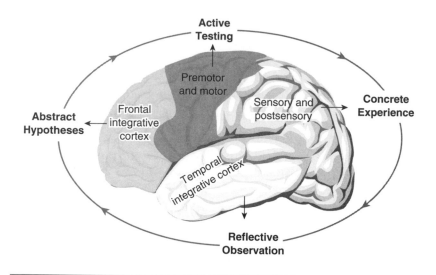

SOURCE: From Zull, J. E. (2002). *The Art of Changing the Brain: Enriching Teaching by Exploring the Biology of Learning.* Copyright © James E. Zull. Published by Stylus Publishing, LLC. Reprinted with permission of the author.

from the new sensory data and links these to prior experience and understanding. The second integrative region, located in the front of the brain, manipulates and transforms the fresh input into new representations, such as abstract ideas, hypotheses, or options for action. This region of the brain/mind, often termed the frontal lobes, is the seat of our executive functions (more on these later). Finally, the motor cortex directs activities to carry out the plans and ideas created by the executive functions. Figure 3.1 shows these regions, with each stage of the natural learning cycle placed adjacent to the relevant brain structure. Table 3.1 summarizes the processes and purposes in each of the biological and learning stages.

The simple, linear nature of our instinctive mental models leads us to think of these stages as sequential—experience, then reflect, then abstract, then test. At best, we might add that the sequence loops, putting "then repeat" at the end of the chain. The research shows, however, that the stages actually interact and feed back in a much richer, more dynamic, and utterly nonlinear fashion, much of which happens beyond our conscious awareness. Figure 3.1 would be more accurate if there were many curvy lines weaving between each of the four regions of the brain and the four stages of the cycle.

Table 3.1

Important functions of each part of the cortex	Matched stages of the learning cycle
The sensory cortex receives first input from the outside world in the form of vision, hearing, touch, position, smells, and taste.	This matches with the common definition of concrete experience with its reliance on direct physical information from the world.
The back integrative cortex is engaged in memory formation and reassembly, language comprehension, developing spatial relationship, and identifying objects, faces, and motion. In short, It Integrates sensory information to create images and meaning.	These functions match well with what happens during reflection—for example, remembering relevant information, daydreaming and free association, developing insights and associations, mentally rerunning experiences, and analyzing experiences.
The frontal integrative cortex is responsible for short-term memory, problem solving, making decisions, assembling plans for action, assembly of language, making judgments and evaluations, directing the action of the rest of the brain (including memory recall), and organizing actions and activities of the entire body.	This matches well with the generation of abstractions, which requires manipulation of images and language to create new (mental) arrangements, developing plans for the future action, comparing and choosing options, directing recall of past experience, creating symbolic representations, and replacing and manipulating items held in short-term memory.
The motor cortex directly triggers all coordinated and voluntary muscle contractions by the body, producing movement. It carries out the plans and ideas originated from the front integrative cortex, including the actual production of language through speech and writing.	This matches with the necessity for action in completion of the learning cycle. Active testing of abstractions requires conversion of ideas into physical action, or movements of parts of the body. This includes intellectual activities such as writing, deriving relationships, doing experiments, and talking in debate or conversation.

SOURCE: From Zull, J. E. (2002). *The Art of Changing the Brain: Enriching Teaching by Exploring the Biology of Learning.* Copyright © James E. Zull. Published by Stylus Publishing, LLC. Reprinted with permission of the author.

BRAIN/MIND BASICS

Scientific research into the workings of the brain and human cognition expanded dramatically in scope over the past few decades, resulting in an immense body of scholarly papers and a very large library of thorough yet very readable surveys (e.g., Begley, 2007; Gardner, 1985, 1993; Goleman, 2006; Gopnik, Meltzoff, & Kuhl, 1999).

The translation of key findings from this research into practical guidance for other professional fields is also expanding. In education, a number of authors and researchers have traced the importance that modern neuroscience has for the design of effective learning environments and teaching practices (e.g., National Research Council, 1999; Caine & Caine, 1991; Hart, 1998; Jensen, 1995; Restak, 2003; Sylwester, 2005; Zull, 2002). These works, individually and together, demonstrate clearly that the scientific evidence is more than sufficient to justify significant change in educational practice. It is thus both surprising and unfortunate that mainstream education has not embraced these findings.

What do we mean when we use the term *brain/mind*? Brain/mind, as coined by Caine and Caine (1991), encompasses human emotions, movement, creativity, and immune responses, as well as the ability to use language to reason, plan, organize, and dream. Other terms are sometimes used to convey this and related meanings, such as *brain-based, brain-compatible,* or *body-brain*. We follow this definition here, using the word *brain* alone only in contexts where it is important to draw a focus on the biological brain itself.

> The brain/mind, as a living system, is a complex set of richly interacting elements that always operate in concert.

It is important to gain a basic grasp of this scientific work before moving on to examine the translation of it into practical guidance for educators and leaders. We find that five major points serve effectively as lenses that help focus on the findings that are most important for school leaders to bear in mind. Again, we emphasize that the linear structure of this summary reflects the linear nature of a book, not the priority or relationship of the brain/mind characteristics described. The brain/mind, as a living system, is a complex set of richly interacting elements that always operate in concert. Each and all of these principles are operative simultaneously, all of the time.

The Brain/Mind Is a Complex Living System

Though the brain is a distinct physical organ, it is not disconnected from the body as the common mind-body dichotomy implies. It is "as much a part of our body as is our liver," notes biologist James Zull (2002). Millions of sensory circuits allow the brain to continually sense what is happening in and around the body. Other millions of cellular pathways carry signals from the brain that command bodily movement and other processes. The brain and other parts of the body also produce and exchange chemicals that carry important messages about their current state. Although slower than the cellular signals, these chemical messengers play very important roles in brain/mind processes. The bottom line is simple but far-reaching in its consequences: Everything that affects our brain affects our body. It turns out that the reverse is also true.

Experiences Sculpt the Brain Physically

Every human brain starts with about the same number of cells and the same gross structure. Beginning in the womb, every stimulus, interaction, and experience produces a physical alteration in the brain—each one literally resculpts the brain's physiology. This is true of physical experiences and social interactions as well as intellectual or purely mental experiences. The specific pattern of pathways in each brain becomes totally unique as a result, which is perhaps the most fundamental way in which no two individuals are alike. Frequently repeated or sustained stimulus triggers the development of new neurons and new pathways among brain regions; with lack of use, they are pruned away.

Experience shows that we learn more readily when we're younger. This mental limberness reflects the plasticity of the brain, or neuroplasticity. This declines with age, and it used to be thought that it died out altogether at a fairly early age. Beyond that point, the brain was believed to be hardwired, its structure frozen. The new research has shown otherwise, with conclusive evidence that the brain remains plastic as long as it's alive. "You can't teach an old dog new tricks" will have to be replaced with something like, "Even old dogs can learn a few new tricks"!

Making Meaning Is Innate and Automatic

The brain is hardwired to identify the meaning of new sensory input and recognize what actions must be taken as a consequence. This essential survival function is automatic and operating all the time, though we're usually not conscious of it. The regions and pathways responsible for this innate, automatic process operate several times faster than those involved in conscious thought, allowing our vital survival reactions to act as quickly as possible.

> The brain is hardwired to identify the meaning of new sensory input and recognize what actions must be taken as a consequence.

The brain's capacity to make meaning is *primal.* This word carries two important meanings. The first meaning relates to physiology and tells us that the structures and pathways involved develop first within the brain. The second has to do with priority. This survival-related function is of higher importance than other cognitive processes. Social capacity and emotion, which we'll touch on next, are also primal capacities of the brain/mind, first to develop and of first importance.

Making meaning is an integrative and creative process; the brain constructs meaning. Many regions and functions of the brain are involved, including our senses, emotions, and thoughts. The brain works on many levels—on parts and on the whole—simultaneously in seeking and constructing meaning.

The Brain Is Social

Specialized neurons and pathways in the brain underlie the human urge to connect with others and our capacity for rapport and empathy. Operating below the level of conscious awareness, these "interpersonal radar" circuits (Goleman, 2006) process several times faster than conscious thoughts. They allow us to understand the messages contained in other people's body language, gestures, and actions without conscious thought. They are vital to our survival. The attraction between mates, the parent–child bond, and the ability to sense threat from another human all rely on these intimate brain-to-brain links.

The key to these capacities is a special class of neurons called *mirror neurons*. As the name implies, mirror neurons enable us to perceive, understand, and mirror the emotional states of others. Researchers' understanding of how mirror neurons work has grown tremendously over the past decade (Goleman, 2006; Pert, 1997). The new insights shed light on a number of phenomena of interest to teachers and leaders. One of these is emotional contagion. Ever notice how quickly a happy mood changes when someone comes into the room with an angry scowl on his face? Research confirms that just seeing the outward sign of this stressful, perhaps threatening, emotional state actually changes the inward emotional state of the observer. Mirror neurons initiate this change, which occurs much faster than the conscious reactions of sitting up straighter or pretending to study the notepad on the table.

Imitative learning is another capacity linked to mirror neurons and important in both the conference room and the classroom. *Imitation*, another word for mirroring, is an innate function of the brain/mind. Without conscious intent, humans imitate the behaviors and habits, language, and values of others who belong to social groups that are important to them.

One of the most startling results of modern research is that motor functions are also activated by observation. While it was obvious that physical repetition of a task patterned the brain/mind and produced better performance, scientists believed the reverse could not be true. In other words, just watching someone else perform a task, or imagining the doing of it, would not sculpt the brain the way a physical action would. Brain-imaging studies from research conducted during "The Decade of the Brain"[1] have revealed that the patterning does indeed occur in both directions (Rizzolatti & Craighero, 2004). The same brain circuits are triggered, including motor cortex circuits, when we observe or visualize an action as when we actually do it. Athletes and actors who use visualization to improve their performances would attest to the truth of this, and now the physiological basis is clear.

---

[1] A 10-year initiative from 1990 to 1999 to educate Congress and the public about brain research and its mental health implications.

Emotions Are Primal

New research sheds important light on two vital topics: the interplay of emotion with cognition and the important role emotion plays in learning. The duality of emotion and intellect has intrigued and bewildered humans as far back as history records. Since ancient times, we've drawn on the familiar experience of domesticated animals for metaphors that could capture the often unsteady balance between the calm and cool of our rational mind and our unruly fears and passions. Author Jonathan Haidt (2006) used the vivid and engaging metaphor of a young boy riding an elephant. The boy (representing the executive functions, or our rational, intellectual mind) guides the elephant along his intended route, constantly scanning his surroundings and making adjustments needed to avoid traffic jams or skirt hazards. As long as nothing spooks the elephant (the emotions) into a rampage, the boy will proceed happily along his route, no doubt taking pride in the excellent plan he made and his remarkable riding skills. In reality, though, the outcome always depends mainly on the elephant's staying calm. Emotions are primal: They inhibit or overwhelm the higher executive functions.

> *Individuals with highly developed executive functions have mastered the ability to plan and organize their thinking, use reason, engage in risk management, make sense of ideas and behavior, multitask, moderate emotions, work with longer time horizons, think critically, access working memory, and reflect on their own strengths and weaknesses.* (Caine, Caine, McClintic, & Klimek, 2004, p. 7)

Metaphors like this remind us of the human mind's natural tendency to form very simple models to help it make sense of complex experiences. Casting emotion and intellect into a tidy dichotomy—as if one can choose to be either intellectual or emotional and can prevent the two modalities from intermingling—is just such a conveniently simple model. But it's a false dichotomy: The elephant and the boy are both essential participants in the same journey, and the behavior of each affects both the next actions of the other and their shared journey. They are inextricably linked, each an integral part of a living system.

Within the human brain, emotion and intellect are intimately intertwined and active in all cognitive processes. The human brain has no pathway for sensory input that bypasses its emotional processing functions. Purely rational, intellectual cognition is impossible for the brain. The neuronal circuitry that triggers emotional processing centers fires much faster than does the circuitry for higher-order processing (Goleman, 2006). This means that it is the brain/mind's emotional circuits that determine whether or not our executive functions will prevail in any given circumstance.

TEACHING, LEARNING, AND LEADING

Two other notable trailblazers in the quest to understand how knowledge of the brain/mind could inform teaching and learning are Geoffrey and Renate Caine. Like Kolb and Zull, they too examined a vast body of research, ranging from clinical and cognitive psychology to biology and neuroscience. The Caines, however, focused specifically on integrating these diverse bodies of research for the purpose of improving teaching and learning in schools.

Their goal was to identify principles that could be correlated with classroom needs and translated into practical methods for educators. The dictionary reminds us that *principle* means a "fundamental, primary, or general law or truth from which other (rules) are derived." In other words, not every interesting or important idea qualifies as a principle. Renate Caine identified four criteria that a concept or finding would have to meet if it truly was a principle (Caine, in press):

- *The phenomena described by the principle should be universal.*
  A principle must refer to phenomena that are true for all human beings, despite individual genetic variations, unique expressions, and developmental differences.
- *Research documenting any one specific principle should span more than one field or discipline.*
  Triangulation through research across multiple fields and disciplines must confirm that a principle is valid and truly describes a systems property.
- *A principle should anticipate future research.*
  A principle must be able to accommodate and account for the new information and fresh perspectives that

emerge continually from ongoing research, inquiry, and experience.

- *The principle should provide implications for practice.*
  A principle is, by definition, a general statement that cannot be expected to give practitioners explicit, step-by-step instructions. It should, however, provide the basis for an effective general framework to guide decisions and to help in the identification and selection of appropriate methods and strategies.

Guided by these four criteria, the Caines identified 12 brain/mind learning principles (Caine & Caine, 1991). Through further research and practice, they identified key characteristics (which they call "capacities") that learning environments must have in order to activate the learning principles as fully as possible. Each capacity correlates with one of the principles, thus making a direct tie back to attributes of the brain/mind that are now well established by scientific research. The capacities are very practical entry points to the research for everyone whose work touches the learning experience, from building architects to teachers, curriculum specialists to administrators.

We have found that the simplest and most powerful bridge between the Caines's work on learning and our current focus on leadership lies in the three interactive teaching elements that emerge from the 12 principles (see Figure 6.7). Let's look more carefully at the link between leading and learning.

Generative leaders recognize that every person in their school or organization is actually learning all the time. This is true whether the person's role is student, principal, teacher, or coach and whether the challenge is to do an experiment, research a question, or improve administrative processes. They know that each person will be most effective in his or her role when conditions allow the brain/mind to access the full range of its capacities. In a sense, then, generative school leaders see that leading effective learning is at the very core of their job. They recognize that learning is not merely an intellectual task but a process

> Generative leaders recognize that every person in their school or organization is actually learning all the time.

that always involves the entire brain, including its primal emotional and social functions.

The interactive teaching elements that emerge from the Caines's principles serve the generative school leader as powerful lenses through which to examine the environment and processes in which both adults and students are operating.

Relaxed Alertness

Relaxed alertness is the optimal state for learning. It conveys the central role that emotions play in learning, either enabling or shutting off access to the higher processing regions of the brain. *Relaxed* signals a supportive social context that provides physical and emotional safety. *Alertness* signals anticipation and active awareness.

What we know about learning with students is also true for adults: Adults will converse, create, plan, inquire, and build relationships more meaningfully and effectively in environments that are high challenge/low threat—where the relaxed alert state is the norm. Generative leaders consider the principles and capacities that influence relaxed alertness as they guide their school's culture and design systems and processes. They know that creativity will flourish and their staff will work more effectively and efficiently, with purpose and intent, in a relaxed/alert climate.

Orchestrated Immersion/Complex Experience

The human brain learns through experience, which it receives through the senses. The brain learns by making connections between what is experienced and what that experience means to the learner. An enriched or "complex" environment, one that engages the physical senses and fosters the use of the integrative and executive functions, is optimal for learning. *Immersion* signals rich sensory input, and *orchestrated* signals intentional design and guidance of the immersion to maximize purposeful learning.

Active, in-depth experiences are as important for adults as they are for students. Think back to some time when a staff meeting or presentation required no meaningful involvement from you, physically, emotionally, or intellectually. Try to remember how that felt and how little insight or productivity you could generate. The generative leader strives to design experiences that activate multiple brain/mind pathways and immerse adults in deep conversations, reflection, and learning. They understand that these experiences foster the creativity and productivity that are crucial to their school's future.

Active Processing

The processing of experience completes the natural learning cycle, for adults as well as children. It is how we make personal sense of new information and learn in depth. Active processing activates and develops the more complex functions of the brain/mind, including the executive functions.

Active processing ranges from systematic practice and creative rehearsal (for memory recall) to the real-world experiences and deep probing of questions that test how well the learner can put new knowledge to new uses. For adults, reflection, conversation, group processes, even drawing and creating visual summaries of conversations, provide ways to consolidate new ideas and stimulus with their prior knowledge and experience. The generative leader understands that such activities are essential stages in effective learning and provides the time and opportunity for them to occur.

IMPLICATIONS FOR LEADERS

Generative leaders know that continual learning is essential to the vitality and success of their organization. Generative school leaders recognize that this is true not only in the classroom but also throughout the dynamic system that is their school. They develop a solid understanding of brain/mind science, focusing on how the brain/mind learns naturally and how contextual factors can support or inhibit rich creativity and effective learning. Looking at both the classroom and the meeting room as learning environments, they ensure that each provides the relaxed alertness, orchestrated immersion/complex experiences, and active processing needed for optimal learning.

RECAP

The brain is a parallel processor designed to make meaning of sensory experience. It processes both parts (specific stimulus) and wholes (meanings, ideas, patterns, actions) simultaneously.

Emotion and social interactions are primal functions of the brain: among the first brain structures to develop physically and of first importance in all cognition. Positive emotion and social interaction circumstances enable and enhance learning and relationships. Conversely, ambiguous, threatening, or painful circumstances trigger primal circuits that overwhelm learning and higher cognitive functions.

No cognitive pathways bypass the brain's emotion and social circuitry. *interconnectedness*

Zull has shown that Kolb's four stages of experiential learning—concrete experience, reflective observation, abstract hypotheses and active testing—correlate with four anatomical regions of the cortex (the outer sheath of the brain). The four brain regions process sensory stimulus, integrate it into meaning and then abstract ideas and, finally, direct actions. All four stages and regions are active and interacting together simultaneously as we learn.

Experience equals learning, and learning sculpts the brain physically. The brain is more plastic—easier to sculpt—when we are young, but retains some plasticity throughout life.

The weight of neuroscience and related education research is more than sufficient to warrant comprehensive incorporation in mainstream educational practice; this has yet to happen.

A concise and rigorous set of brain/mind principles for effective teaching and learning has been identified. They can guide the design of effective learning environments and classroom practice and are also directly relevant for school leaders.

The three interactive elements that emerge from these principles—Relaxed Alertness, Orchestrated Immersion/Complex Experience and Active Processing—effectively bridge leadership to brain/mind research and are powerful touchstones for generative leaders.

To lead is to learn, and the essence of generative leadership is generative learning. Everything we understand about learning and the brain/mind thus applies to effective leadership.

REFLECTIONS

- Brain/mind research is typically focused on teaching and learning. How does this information inform your role as a generative leader? How might you see differently the importance of identity, information, and relationships within your school through the lens of brain/mind research? How could this knowledge challenge your assumptions about a new future for your school?

- Can you recall a time when you experienced the complete natural learning cycle in a spontaneous fashion? What did that feel like? Do you see this cycle in action anywhere in your school? What stages of the natural learning cycle have you activated while reading this book?

- Do you see the natural learning cycle in action in your classrooms? How often are they observable in administrative and planning processes? What could you do to strengthen each of the four stages in your personal and professional work?

- How might knowledge of the three interactive teaching elements influence your design of professional development within your school and/or district? How might this information influence your planning of staff meetings, administrative meetings, and/or parent meetings?

- Looking through the lenses of Zull's model of natural learning and the Caines's interactive teaching elements, how might you design opportunities for your staff to narrate, improvise, and be joint authors of the future of your school? To what extent will you monitor how they make meaning from these experiences? How will you know if your staff is emotionally engaged?

Generative School Leadership

4

For the real question is whether the brighter future is really always so distant. What if, on the contrary, it has been here for a long time already, and only our own blindness and weakness has prevented us from seeing it around us and within us, and kept us from developing it?

—Vaçlav Havel, open letter on "The Power of the Powerless" (Havel, 1985)

It is hard to describe generative school leadership in a few simple words. It is not just another clever fix-it technique or a New Age fad, and developing it can't be reduced to a handy "how-to" recipe. It emerges as the understanding of our three foundational elements (generativity, living systems principles, and brain/mind science) deepens and expands into a fundamentally new way of seeing one's school. Seeing with the "new eyes" of generative leadership is powerful, as this chapter's opening quote reminds us. With these new eyes, leaders can see more clearly the full capacity and creativity of their entire school and take steps to tap these more fully. With these new eyes, previously unseen pathways for action are discovered that create new futures for schools.

EXPANDING POSSIBILITIES

Generative school leaders are intent on actualizing the generative capacity of their school for one very simple reason: They realize that both students and staff will learn, perform, and thrive better. Generative environments are rich in stimuli, offering challenges and contrasts to existing mental models that can catalyze new ideas and new avenues for action. Generative leaders push back on the commonplace mechanistic ways of organizing and doing business to make room for generative modes of inquiry and action. The dominant machinelike mental model of our day is unrelenting and impatient in rushing from symptom to analysis to fix. It leaves no time or mental space for inquiry, creativity, and reflection—modes of cognition that are integral stages in learning and essential to breaking out of the blindness of which Havel speaks. Generative school leaders realize that we cannot shape new futures for our schools without the expansive impetus that generativity provides.

They also know that they must highlight and nurture the living systems characteristics of their school in order to grow the generative capacity of their school. They do this by fostering a clear school identity, which they model and express consistently. They ensure that the organizational patterns and processes of their school encourage the active seeking of information and its open exchange on all levels. And they steward a school culture in which authentic human relationships are the norm between and among students, teachers, and staff. They understand that respect and authority are amplified, not eroded, in authentic relationships.

> *Real understanding requires and leads to a shift in one's mental model.* (Caine et al., 2004, p. 73)

Generative leaders create cultures and work processes that support expansive, fertile phases of inquiry on questions that really matter in order to complement the convergent drive of the mechanistic model. They let go of some control (not authority) in order to achieve creativity, collaboration, collective intelligence, and new pathways for action. Four strong positives in exchange for a bit of give is quite a powerful trade!

Last, generative school leaders recognize that the workings of the brain/mind are pivotal in this endeavor. They are constantly mindful of the how the brain learns naturally, and they work tirelessly to ensure that student and staff activities support the entire learning cycle whenever possible. They understand that making meaning is the automatic, natural function of the brain/mind and realize the primal role that emotions have in all human cognition. The generative school leader knows that relaxed alertness is the state of mind that supports optimal learning, and he or she works tirelessly to ensure that the physical environment, the school culture, and work processes foster this state for staff and students alike.

THE LOOK AND FEEL OF GENERATIVITY

What does generative leadership look like in a real school setting? Let's consider an example from a high school in the Midwest. The principal of this school, a senior administrator, schooled herself in living systems principles and brain/mind science for many years, first exploring their implications for the classroom and later for staff challenges. She avidly sought new insights about leadership from outside the realm of education and tested these in her own leadership work. When the opportunity arose to form and lead a new school, she seized it eagerly. There was one nonnegotiable condition: She intended to be a generative leader and to shape the entire school environment in this fashion from the very start. This excerpt from an essay written by someone at the school provides a glimpse of what being there looks and feels like:

> The culture here is different from more "traditional" schools. We pride ourselves in being a high challenge and low threat place, but this doesn't mean just taking AP classes or knowing the right answer. It also doesn't mean being "loosey-goosey." We have expectations for everyone, both students AND the staff—and many of them are the same for all of us. The expectations set the stage for how we work and behave here . . . they're really our rules. They're up on the wall in several areas of the building so that we can see them every day. We care about each other. We're all connected, and we all want to learn. We explore, take

risks, make mistakes. We create—in science class and math class and the computer lab—and in staff meetings. There's a great deal of talk in this school and a good deal of laughing. We like to try on ideas and see how they play out with the others. We ask lots of questions. We listen to each other. You don't see someone barking out orders or commands—our common purpose and commitments are so clear that this kind of "being in charge" isn't needed. All of the students do research here, all year and every year. On research days, we're everywhere—in the gym, in the old cafeteria, in labs, hallways and makeshift "research rooms," gathering data. The whole school is sort of like a professional lab— messy, sometimes noisy, sometimes smelly. Teachers watch the students do research and ask each other questions, so that they can help one another answer the ones from student research teams. Everyone here is friendly and supports each other. With the couches and the plants and kites hanging and the freedom that we have, it's more like a college atmosphere than a typical high school. People who come to visit tell us that they don't want to leave. It's comfortable here. We know it's our school, and we can make it what we wish. You have to pay attention to everything that's happening and give a lot of energy to make schools like this work, but it's worth it.

Imagine being a guest who has just walked into this school for the first time. What do you think you would see and hear? What parts of the description do you find familiar? Are some puzzling, some appalling? Do some questions come immediately to your mind? Who in the school would you approach about your perceptions and questions?

Questions like these can lead to valuable insights about the assumptions embedded in your current mental models— the simplified concepts of "student" and "teacher," "principal" or "leader"—that operate continuously in your unconscious, filtering and evaluating new information, such as this vignette of a high school. This chapter will invite you to reflect on questions like these, think differently about your role and methods as a leader, and look anew at the patterns and networks that embody and reflect the living system characteristics of your

Many of today's most creative and successful companies are famous for being like this—high-challenge, low-threat environments that are rich in conversation and have creative, playful atmospheres.

school. The three foundational elements explored in the preceding chapters will be tightly interwoven here, as they are in nature and in generative leadership.

We all know that the kind of vibrant, creative work environment sketched in this school vignette can and does exist. Many of today's most creative and successful companies are famous for being like this—high-challenge, low-threat environments that are rich in conversation and have creative, playful atmospheres. Their leaders don't just allow such a generative environment to exist; they work very intentionally to create and sustain it. Designing an appealing physical work environment is the smallest piece of this challenge. By far the most important task of the leader in highly successful innovative companies is to foster and sustain a culture that is wide open to information, welcoming to new ideas, and safe for individual creativity. These leaders put a high premium on culture and environment for one very simple and utterly practical reason: The survival and success of their organization depends on their team's continual learning, creativity, and innovation.

Few schools today fit this picture of a workplace culture. Most are locked firmly into mechanistic structures and centered on practices designed to maintain rigid control. Walking into a school like this, one often senses the dampened energy of an audit compliance culture. Sadder still, it seems that many educators and administrators believe it's impossible for schools to change in this more generative direction. A long list of reasons is given for why this is so, including the uniqueness of education as an enterprise, the intense public scrutiny and demands for accountability that schools face, budgetary pressures, or the behavioral challenges arising from the short-term focus and consumerism of today's techno-media saturated society.

Education in schools could hardly be more unrealistic. Students, when they are given a problem, can usually assume they have been taught everything needed to solve the problem. How many of you in your own affairs find that challenges come pre-equipped with everything for a solution? (Forrester, 1996, p. 5)

These and many other factors certainly make school leadership today a very complex challenge. Yet some schools—public and private, large and small—do work in a generative fashion. And within any single school, one can almost always find one or two teachers whose classrooms are shining examples of generative learning environments, no matter how dauntingly different the overall school or administrative culture might be. The difference is always leadership: the generative leadership capacity and drive of an individual within the school.

A LENS ON LEARNING

We cannot understand generative school leadership without first considering the learning environment. Sustaining a high-quality and effective learning environment is every school leader's most important responsibility. The previous vignette gives us some important clues about the kind of environment, culture, and instructional practices fostered by generative school leaders:

We pride ourselves in being a high challenge and low threat place . . .

. . . we explore, take risks, make mistakes. We create . . .

There's a great deal of talk in this school and a good deal of laughing . . .

We like to try on ideas and see how they play out with the others . . .

We ask lots of questions. We listen to each other . . .

. . . students do research . . .

. . . "being in charge" isn't needed . . .

The ties back to key principles of living systems and brain/mind science are clearly traceable in these words. There's a clear sense of shared school identity and an awareness of self-organization at work. Information is avidly sought and openly shared among and between staff and students. The relationship pathways in this school are authentic, comfortable, and valued. All these testify that a healthy living system dynamic prevails in this school.

The culture and emotional climate in the school are "high challenge and low threat," allowing both students and teachers to function in the relaxed alertness state that is optimal for learning. It is clear from these words that constructivist practices are the norm at this school. Examples of experience, reflection, abstraction, and testing are abundant. These indicate that orchestrated immersion and active processing are woven into the fabric of teaching and learning, which ensures that all four stages of natural learning are activated consistently.

Look at the action language in this vignette: *explore, take risks, try on new ideas, make mistakes*. These indicate that generative learning is indeed happening in this school. Recall that generative learning emphasizes continuous experimentation, systematic thinking, and a willingness to creatively explore the limits of an issue and to think creatively outside its limits.

LEADERSHIP MODALITIES

The principal who leads the high school sketched earlier is a generative leader. Her intention to sustain a generative culture throughout the school guides how even general administrative matters are handled. Her focus on drawing out the energy and capacity of the students, teachers, and administrators around her shifts the character of virtually every interaction and shapes the outwardly apparent culture of the entire school. The school system in which she works is a very typical one, however. Her school is not exempt from any of the usual expectations and deliverables. Most people within the district, and even some within her own school, have no concept of generative leadership. How did this principal become a generative leader? Now that she leads in this fashion, how does she relate to the environment around her and ensure her students and her school succeed?

One place to start exploring these questions is with the concept of leadership itself and the approaches to leading one often sees in practice. Countless books and professional articles describe styles of leadership and offer models or frameworks of varying complexity to capture them. Our many decades of practice in challenging environments led us to a simpler synthesis of four modalities. Each of these fuses together the three foundational elements of generativity, living systems principles, and brain/mind principles. Moving from the least generative to the most generative, these are *traditional leadership, pragmatic leadership, explorative leadership,* and *generative leadership.*

> Our many decades of practice in challenging environments led us to a simpler synthesis of four modalities.

Traditional

Traditional leaders typically do as was done before. Their repertoire of techniques draws primarily from history and the patterns already embedded in the school's practices and culture. Decision making tends to be quite prescriptive, with preference for consistency and stability. "By-the-book" is a norm for everything, from daily operations to curriculum implementation and annual planning. These leaders see their primary role as maintaining order and consistency and ensuring compliance with standards and methods approved by other authorities. The style of traditional leaders is usually hierarchical, with the top administrator making decisions and subordinates taking directions. The culture surrounding a traditional leader is typically one of control and compliance.

Pragmatic

Pragmatic leaders focus on keeping things going smoothly. They don't seek innovation unless necessary, as when change is forced on them by new circumstances or requirements. They cope with such forces by finding the modest incremental changes needed to restore things to "normal" stability and consistency. Successful past practices serve as the starting point for identifying these adaptive fixes. This leadership style is predominantly top-down hierarchical, with input from subordinates sometimes accepted when developing the changes needed to meet the new situations. The culture surrounding this leader is conservative and focused on stability of the status quo.

Explorative

Explorative leaders bring an active curiosity to their tasks. Their nature is to look continually beyond their school and their own selves for fresh ideas, better approaches, and new opportunities. They pursue new ideas actively by asking questions of colleagues at all levels, seeking chances to attend workshops, and keeping abreast of experiments in teaching and learning throughout the field. Questioning ideas—even one of their ideas—is seen as constructive exploration rather than as insubordination. Their style tends to be consultative, welcoming ideas and questions from internal participants and external sources. They are always authoritative but authoritarian in manner only when specific circumstances require them to be so. The explorative leader fosters a culture of curiosity and inquiry, with some latitude for independent action.

Generative

Generative leaders see their school as a dynamic system that is being co-created through the interactions of all its participants internally and with the outside environment. They emphasize systems thinking consistently. They question the assumptions and presumed limits of an issue that are embedded in the prevailing mental models. Generative leaders aim to release the creativity and fulfill the potential of everyone connected to the school, not just to control their time and energy. They foster an environment of continual experimentation in which creativity and innovation can flourish. The future—from the very next moment to what their school could become a year or two onward—is the primary reference for these leaders. They focus on the actions needed to attain an envisioned future rather than the fixes needed to restore equilibrium. The culture surrounding a generative leader is a co-creative one, in which every individual is confident that he or she is valued, empowered, and authorized to contribute creatively to shaping the system and its future.

A DEVELOPMENTAL CONTINUUM

The principal in our high school example was a rather traditional leader early in her career, when she first became an administrator. Most of the school leaders for whom she had worked operated primarily in this modality, and what little formal training she received in "school management" was rooted in it as well. Continual study and reflection and experimentation throughout her career progressively shaped her into the generative leader she is today. She has a deep understanding of each of the modalities, and her rich repertoire of skills and techniques includes elements from all of them. She is both traditional and explorative, both practical and generative, depending on the situation and even the individual she is dealing with.

> A generative leader creates the environment where people can do their best thinking, by challenging habitual mindsets and limiting old scripts. By removing barriers that can hamper the birth of innovative ideas and promoting the acquisition of new information and perspectives, meetings become more meaningful and effective. The added dimension of reflective time promotes deep inquiry and can unearth spin-off ideas not initially suggested. (Edwards, 2007, p. 3)

Music again provides a helpful analogy that illustrates some subtle but important points about how the four modalities relate to each other. Novice musicians work hard to master the mechanics of their instruments as well as the challenge of reading the sheet music in front of them. Gaining decent fluency with a set of fairly simple tunes is quite a feat. The virtuoso musician's complete mastery of the instrument and sensitivity to the musical score let her play much more complex pieces brilliantly. While the virtuoso can play one of the novice's simple tunes quite easily, the novice cannot play the virtuoso's symphony. Similarly, a generative or an explorative leader can reach back, as it were, to the perspectives or methods of traditional or practical leadership and use them as needed. But a leader whose practice is anchored in the traditional or practical mode must grow into the explorative and generative modes.

Dedication, passion, learning, and practice are essential ingredients in this growth, for leaders as well as musicians, which highlights the final, crucial point about the four modalities: The sequence from traditional to generative reflects a progression of individual learning and development. Deep personal commitment to continual learning, exploration, innovation, and practice is needed to move along this progression.

As a leader grows and becomes more fluent in this fusion, generative leadership evolves from being a method that is applied deliberately to something more like a guiding philosophy or a way of being. It emerges fully only through practice and continual personal growth.

THE LEADER'S ROLE

Generative leadership is expansive. Questioning common-sense assumptions or limits and welcoming creativity brings to light avenues for action and prospects for the future that were unrecognized before.

The central task of generative leaders is to create an environment that is open to such questioning and innovation, one in which the living system properties of identity, information, and relationships all flourish. They consistently model, encourage, and protect these vital qualities. They lead the school team and community to define identity and envision their shared future.

> Metaphorically, the generative leader creates a container that can hold safely the rich mix of inquiry, creativity, and experimentation that generativity requires. This may occur at the scale of a single classroom or an entire school, depending on the leader's sphere of influence.

The common actions of a traditional leader are to *organize, assign, direct, monitor, correct, verify.* These words all connote the direction of efforts to maintain or restore order and structure. What, then, are the common actions of a generative leader? They are to *question, stimulate, envision, explore, influence,* and *guide.* In other words, generative leaders interact with the living system they are part of, stimulating its intrinsic intelligence and creativity, bringing to light false assumptions that might block ideas and actions and allowing room for self-organization to occur. If identity and purpose are clear, the ideas, solutions, and actions that emerge from such generative processes will be both creative and productive.

On first blush, this vignette of a generative leader's modalities may strike some as too soft or vague to be an effective way of operating. School leaders must get things done, after all, and ensure that myriad deliverables are produced on time. As was pointed out earlier in this chapter, leading generatively does not mean dropping altogether the more traditional modes of action. This is not a case of "either/or" but of "both/and." With both generative and traditional leadership capacities, our schools can have the vibrancy of a living system, the creative capacity needed to remain resilient in the face of constant change, and the high effectiveness that is legitimately expected of them.

THE LEADER'S JOURNEY

No shortcuts to increased mastery exist in either music or leadership, but one can identify important focal points for study and practice. Six hallmarks distinguish experienced generative leaders. These also serve as valuable comparators for those who are just setting out on their journey of development. Our Tools and Resources section (Chapter 6) expands each of these, sharpening the focus on the three fundamental elements (generativity, living systems principles, and brain/mind learning) and providing specific pointers on putting them into practice.

The generative school leader

- Deepens personal knowledge
- Engages in personal reflection
- Promotes professional conversations
- Blends living systems theory with practice
- Relies on creativity and innovation
- Leads toward a desired state

Deepens Personal Knowledge

Generative leaders are eager and continual learners. They aspire to always be a rich source of new information and incisive questions. Therefore, they challenge existing knowledge and assumptions of a group to bring new possibilities to the fore. They avidly seek new knowledge and explore differing perspectives with genuine curiosity.

Engages in Personal Reflection

Generative leaders understand that reflection is a vital process in natural learning and is essential to creativity and innovation. They know that natural reflection is not just an intellectual function of the brain. It involves a rich interplay of emotion, intuition, and sensory input as well as cognition. They make time to put aside thoughts about the workday's data and events and to exercise and play with their other cognitive and sensory functions.

Promotes Professional Conversations

Generative leaders know that conversation is the lifeblood of their school, carrying its vital information and nourishing the authentic relationships that will allow it to thrive. They foster and support informal conversations, knowing that these can be important stages in the natural learning cycles of staff and students alike. Recognizing that conversation is the earliest and still most powerful of human social technologies, they place authentic conversation at the core of all administrative processes, from staff meetings to budgeting and planning.

Blends Living Systems Theory With Practice

Generative leaders "see" their school through the prism of living systems rather than as a machine. They understand it is a complex, dynamic, self-organizing system whose vital properties are identity, information, and relationships. They put this understanding into practice in every interaction, from a one-to-one encounter with a student to staff meetings and initiatives.

Relies on Creativity and Innovation

Generative leaders realize that creativity and innovation—the making of new meaning and new connections—are essential functions of the brain. They reject the common notion that creativity and innovation are things one does only in designated periods or once a year as a token step in planning. They understand that both are vital to the learning of staff as well as students and are the cornerstones of an effective school culture. Generative leaders strive to keep their energies focused on creativity and innovation, no matter what challenge is before them.

Envisions and Leads Toward a Desired State

Generative leaders are keenly aware of the continual dance they are in with their present capacity, the emerging conditions that surround them, and the future that lies before them.

SITUATIONAL ASSESSMENTS

Looking at your school through new eyes will help you develop awareness of two vitally important factors that generative leaders monitor continuously. The first of these is your own generative capacity. Do you recognize generativity in the day-to-day language, actions, and behaviors of your teachers, staff, and students? Can you discern the interplay of living systems and brain/mind functions that are active in each instance? The second key factor is the state of your school itself as an organization. Where is generativity common and thriving? Where does it seem absent? Keen observation and reflection will give you a good sense of how your own generative capacity relates to that of your school; it will point the way toward productive starting points for further individual growth and advancing leadership practice.

10 OPERATIONAL INDICATORS

To "look with new eyes" means to look again at something very familiar but with an alertness to features or characteristics that have not typically been the focus of attention. Through interviews and observations in myriad schools and our own leadership practice, we have identified 10 operational indicators that are useful in assessing how generatively a leader or an organization is behaving. The indicators highlight behaviors and qualities that one can readily observe or hear as one visits a school, watches a staff meeting, or talks with the people working and learning there. You can watch for them in your own leadership work, using them as barometers of your growing generative capacity. Finally, you might also use the indicators as points for reflection in keeping with the natural learning cycle described in Chapter 3. Depending on your circumstances, this might be an individual reflective process or something you can share with a group of colleagues or a work team.

It is important not to approach these as a menu of possible choices, thinking that the aim is to choose just one or two and drop the rest. We name them and list them individually by necessity—books are linear creations that force such structures into ideas. In reality, these behaviors and qualities combine holistically, each one inseparable from all the others and together composing a rich web of interactions and feedback. They are all vibrantly active in concert. Of course, this does not mean that each is active in every single setting and at each and every moment. As before, music offers a helpful analogy here: The artistry of a piece of fine music, consisting of many notes and played by many instruments, lies in how the notes and instrumental voices blend and flow in the performance. So it is with generative leadership: Generative leaders develop an acute awareness and judgment for how to blend and adjust these attitudes and behaviors in different circumstances to sustain vitality, creativity, and effectiveness in their schools.

1. **Examining the status quo**

   The status quo is always open to question. "How it's always been," "the way we've always done it," and similar statements do not stop conversation in generative schools. Instead, they tee up fresh questions that all engage with in an open, curious, and eager-to-learn fashion. Asking such questions is not the privilege of one or two titled leaders but the shared activity of faculty, staff, and students alike. Everyone is confident that questioning the status quo is a safe and important thing to do.

2. **Empowerment and responsibility**

   Everyone in the school is empowered to participate in the school's progress and in both individual and collective learning processes. They are also responsible for making constructive contributions to the school. Their formal title or role takes a back seat to their status as an integral element in the living system and a valued individual contributor. So, for example, the professionals on staff are invited and expected to take part in developing a professional development plan that aligns with instructional best practices and meets both school and individual needs. Similarly, teachers give students abundant opportunities to join them in creating classroom projects and programs and hold them accountable for the caliber of their participation and contributions. The school's vision and purpose emerge through a rich collaborative process involving all adults and informed by substantial student participation.

3. **Authenticity and enthusiasm**

   The school environment is one in which staff, students, and parents openly share an authentic and enthusiastic commitment to each other and to the school's vision, values, and success. Authentic relationships exist, making interpersonal contacts richly human rather than transactional. The overall tone of the culture is appreciative and constructive. The behavior of faculty, staff, and students reflect this consistently, in classroom, administrative, and all other school activities.

4. **Respect for physical environment**

   Students, faculty, and staff share ownership and pride of the school facility, grounds, and equipment. Whether these are new or old, meager or fancy, they are respected by all and stewarded with care and respect.

5. **Honor is a two-way street**

   Students and staff respect and support each other, both as school members and as people. The individual talents and capabilities of each member of the learning community are recognized and honored. The authority that goes with formal positions, such as principal or teacher, is respected even when it's not being imposed overtly. Conversely, administrators use their authorities only when and as really needed, never just to reinforce their status above others.

6. **Servant educators**

   The professional and nonprofessional staff, at all levels, see their purpose as serving the students and the school's core purpose. Students and learning come first, not their own individual concerns. They work constructively together to overcome administrative or political challenges rather than allowing these to overwhelm their shared purpose of effective teaching and genuine learning.

7. **Natural learning**

   Brain/mind compatible natural learning is at the core of the school's teaching philosophy and practice and takes priority in curriculum and instructional matters. Decisions and discussions about all learners are grounded in sound research on how learning occurs in the brain/mind. All school leaders collaborate to protect this commitment to learners from the inevitable challenges that arise via budgets and legislative and administrative mandates. Recognizing that the adults in the school are also learning continually, leaders infuse these same principles into the administrative processes.

8. **Context and congruency**

   The learning environment, curriculum, and instructional practices are all truly and richly informed by research-supported brain/mind principles for natural learning, such as those of Caine et al. (2004). Observable indicators of this include curriculum that links closely to the learner's experience(s) and constructivist instructional approaches. The assessments of learning that anchor school accountability are also informed by this research and so include tools that engage all four stages of natural learning.

9. **Parents in the process**

   Organizations with a clear, stable identity tend to be more expansive and more open to genuine engagement with their stakeholders. Parents are vital elements of the learning system, influencing the students through daily conversations at home, in the car, at the ballpark. They endorse and support the work of the school because they understand what is being taught, why it is being taught, how it is being taught, and what their role is in assisting the process of learning.

10. **All leaders are learners**

The school's leaders are avid and humble continual learners, seeking wisdom from experts both within and beyond education. They harvest the lessons learned and the proven methods and insights they discover through their independent study and weave these into their own practice.

RECAP

The fusion of generativity, living systems theory, and brain/mind science gives leaders "new eyes" through which to see their school and their task as a leader. In the early stages of a leader's development, conscious effort is required to observe and act from this new perspective. With practice, it becomes powerfully natural.

Generative leadership is the most expansive and creative of the four basic leadership modalities. It can be strengthened in both individuals and schools through study, reflection, and practical experience.

Generative leadership expands the array of tools available to leaders and the range of possibilities for action available to schools. It does not rule out or replace altogether more traditional modes of leadership and work organization.

A generative leader's primary focal points are these:

• Tapping the intelligence and creativity that exists within the entire school

• Making the invisibles, such as hidden assumptions, visible and open to question

• Posing generative questions rather than imposing directives

Generative questions are ones that foster systemic thinking, trigger examination of limits and commonsense assumptions, and stimulate creative exploration of alternative pathways for action.

Six hallmarks can guide you in growing your own generative capacity and that of your school.

Ten operational indicators, based on readily observable attributes and behaviors, serve as tools to assess the current generative capacity of an individual, a work unit, or a school.

REFLECTIONS

- As you lead from within the system that is your school or organization, how do you influence the actualization of generative capacity?

- What questions are beginning to emerge that will influence generative thinking within your school? How will you and others begin to articulate the questions that matter?

- How will you invite key participants (teachers, support staff, administrators, parents, students) to participate in conversations about questions?

- In what ways are you beginning to relinquish *control* of the emergence of the system while continuing to maintain authority? Where does "both/and" fit for your leadership?

- Where do you currently reside within the leadership modalities? Using the six hallmarks, where might you begin to ask meaningful questions to develop your generative capacity?

- How do you and your staff create an identity, use information, and create relationships? In *traditional* ways? In *pragmatic* ways? In *explorative* ways? In *generative* ways?" How would you document classroom observations or school improvement from the perspective of the modalities? "Who are your *traditional* staff members? *Pragmatic* staff members? *Explorative* staff members? *Generative* staff members?" How might you influence conversations and decision making with the modalities in mind?

- What does your school or organization need to become a culture of continuous experimentation? Who or what will help you move in this direction? How might the 10 operational indicators inform you?

(Continued)

(Continued)

REFLECTIONS

- To lead is to learn. What implications does this knowledge have for you personally? What are you learning about yourself, your understandings, and your feelings about leadership?

(See Chapters 5 and 6 for processes and tools that will help you move forward with these questions.)

Putting Ideas Into Action   5

Methods and Practices
to Develop Generativity

> *All change, even very large and powerful change,
> begins when a few people start talking with one
> another about something they care about. Simple
> conversations held at kitchen tables, or seated on the
> ground, or leaning against doorways are powerful
> means to start influencing and changing our world.*
>
> —Meg Wheatley (2002, p. 9)

The preceding chapters have laid out the foundational elements of generative leadership and provided some basic tools for leaders to work with. Thus far, the tools provided have been suited primarily to equipping individual leaders to assess and develop their generative capacity. The four modalities presented in Chapter 4, for example, can serve as a tool for assessing one's own generative capacity or that of one's school or work group. The six hallmarks can guide actions to deepen understanding of generative leadership and infuse this growing knowledge into leaders' behavior in all school activities.

Greater individual understanding is important, but what about the collective processes of a school? Are there tools or processes that can help shift the modes of thinking within a school and reshape its planning and operational processes? Yes, there are, and we introduce several proven ones in this chapter.

The "social change technologies" that follow range from the elegantly simple but immensely powerful tools for convening effective conversations on questions that really matter to large-scale systemic change processes that can help schools and school communities tackle tough problems and envision constructive futures.

Unless noted otherwise, these tools and processes are "open-source." This means there are no requirements to engage consultants or purchase commercial training materials in order to use them. Open-source also means that new users have blanket permission to adapt them as needed to make them effective in new settings. The tools' originators grant this blanket permission because they know adaptation will be necessary. No method can be effective if it's imposed, cut-and-paste fashion, on a new environment or engaged like a perfunctory exercise.

> Unless noted otherwise, these tools and processes are "open-source."

The principles underlying each of these tools and processes apply universally, but how they are activated and made effective varies in every organization. You will understand and express them in a unique way because of your past experiences and current mental models. How these new approaches gain root and become effective in your school will depend on the school's unique identity (its sense of purpose, of history, and of its future) as well as the dynamic information flows and relationships within it. The only way to gain fluency and power in your use of them is by making meaning of them as new experiences through the four stages of natural learning. This is not just true for the leader; it applies to everyone in your school.

We want to emphasize again that adding these methods to their repertoire does not mean that generative school leaders totally abandon other modes of working. They can be directive in style or organize work in more traditional patterns whenever this is needed. Adding the generative dimension to learning and leading unleashes the intelligence and creativity that exists throughout the school, which expands its capacity and opens new avenues for action.

THE POWER OF AUTHENTIC CONVERSATION

Conversation has been termed "the most ancient and easiest way for people to cultivate the conditions for change" (Wheatley, 2005, p. 3). This seems hard to believe amid the drone of meetings-as-usual and the flood of talk we all face each day. So much of what passes for conversation today is just someone transmitting words blindly toward another person or, from the other side, of being talked at. This is hardly the kind of transaction that can cultivate the conditions for change!

It is also not the kind of interaction the word *conversation* is meant to signify. The Latin roots of the word mean "to live with" or "to turn about with." This captures much better the mutually empathic exchange of meaning and understanding between people that is the true meaning of conversation. Conversation of this type, what we call "authentic conversation," is one of the key ways we forge meaningful links with other people, the vital links that brain/mind science shows we're hardwired to seek and cultivate.

Authentic conversations are essential to social cohesion. They deepen, amplify, speed up, and strengthen the bonds of trust that are vital to group communication, cooperation, and survival. Through authentic conversation, groups propagate their traditions across generations, exchange the stories that confirm their identity, and bring forward the group's collective knowledge and wisdom. These are conversations that truly matter!

> A remarkably common set of practices for fostering constructive group conversations is found across a wide range of cultures, dating back to ancient times.

Authentic conversation is one of the generative leader's most important tools. How are authentic conversations like this convened and facilitated? History and culture offer good guidance. A remarkably common set of practices for fostering constructive group conversations is found across a wide range of cultures, dating back to ancient times. Our forebears clearly didn't need modern technology to develop a keen understanding of human cognition and communication!

ANCIENT LESSONS

The principles of authentic conversation are drawn from the circle, or council. This is an ancient form of meeting that has gathered people together into respectful conversations for thousands of years. It is still intact in some regions of the world but has been lost in many others.

The principles and practices of authentic conversation are woven into many social technologies in use nowadays to foster shared learning and collaborative dialogue on critical organizational and societal issues. This overview of the underlying principles, practices, and agreements is adapted from Baldwin (1994).

Principles

- Have a higher purpose or a deep question to gather around.
- Rotate leadership of the conversation; rank has no meaning in the circle.
- Take responsibility for the circle and for your own behavior.

Practices

- Listen with attention—respecting the learning process and voice of all the members of the group, focused on understanding the speaker's meaning rather than preparing your own remarks.
- Speak with intention—noting what is relevant to the conversation at the moment.
- Pay attention to beginnings and endings—opening and closing the circle with conscious intent and care.

Agreements

- Suspend judgment: Slow down and really listen. Try to understand the other person's meaning and intention.
- Speak only for yourself: Stick with the first-person voice. Offer what you can and ask for what you need.
- Whatever is said in the circle stays in the circle.
- Silence is also part of the conversation. Allow it and honor it.

Meeting in circle is a powerful way to deepen and speed up the development of trust and shared identity in a group. Clearer identity and stronger relationships both contribute to richer, more open flows of information throughout the system.

Circle conversations are designed to elicit the wisdom of the entire group. They provide a clear window into what is known, believed, felt, feared, and hoped for among the individuals learning and working there. This helps leaders discover deeper issues and new connections of knowledge and experience within the school. Valuable inputs to guidance and strategy can come from this practice.

CIRCLES AT SCHOOL

Gathering in circles is a common practice in many effective classrooms, as a means through which to establish a strong sense of community and inform the larger group. Teachers use circle conversations for many purposes, including goal setting, conflict resolution, project planning, idea sharing, and assignment reviews.

The principles of circle can be translated into any vocabulary that works well for each specific context. For example, Jeanne Gibbs (2001) fosters the inclusion of everyone in the classroom through a set of four operating agreements: attentive listening, appreciation/no put downs, right to pass, and mutual respect. Stating these as agreements instead of rules reminds everyone that they are part of a living system and must sustain a personal commitment. Living these agreements creates a safer social environment for everyone, which brain/mind science tells us is essential for relaxed alertness and optimal learning.

One of the greatest benefits that gathering in circle offers is the opportunity for everyone to reflect on his or her own relationship to the topics at hand. Time to consolidate thoughts and listen to the ideas of the group activates every region of the brain and allows rich, natural learning to occur. Like consistent exercise, the use of circle as a regular component of the school day improves the overall learning health of the school.

School staff and administration are slowly beginning to use similar practices, breaking from the traditional staff meeting formats. In these cases, the traditional "business" of the school is handled mainly through memos or e-mail, allowing the time together as a staff to be devoted to deeper discussions about learning, processes, opportunities—and to getting "unstuck!"

WORLD CAFÉ

The World Café is a method for rapidly tapping the collective intelligence of large groups of people. It creates a living network of collaborative dialogue around questions that matter in real-life situations. It is a provocative metaphor . . . as we create our lives, our organizations and our communities we are, in effect, moving among "table conversations" at the World Café (adapted from Brown, J., & Isaacs, D., *World Café Resource Guide,* 2005, p. xviii).

Operating Principles

- Create hospitable space.
- Explore questions that matter.
- Encourage each person's contribution.
- Connect diverse people and ideas.
- Listen together for patterns, insights, and deeper questions.
- Make collective knowledge visible.

Assumptions

- The knowledge and wisdom we need is present and accessible.
- Collective insight evolves from honoring unique contributions, connecting ideas, listening into the middle, noticing deeper themes and questions.
- The intelligence emerges as the system connects to itself in diverse and creative ways.

Practical Matters

The café has a host, who poses the question(s) and stewards the process. Participants break into small groups (four to six people) to discuss one question together, using the principles of circle conversations. The groups are remixed after 15 to 20 minutes, with one person remaining behind to tell the newcomers about the prior conversation. In the space of just a few hours, this allows even large groups of people to engage in multiple rounds of intimate conversation on an important question. The product is a rich array of ideas, connections, principles, and further questions that can inform research, strategy, and planning.

Powerful, simple questions are essential to productive world cafés. For example, a Danish school community began with the question, "What could a good school also be?" Administrators, teachers, parents, and students all took part together. Several café rounds produced a rich set of aspirations and ideas. The next questions in this café were, "What principles are in here that you want to have in your future together? And what else do you want to say about the future based on these ideas?" At the end of the café conversations on these questions, the students proposed "10 commandments for parents," "10 commandments for teachers," and "10 commandments for students," which now guide the school's operations (Toke Moeller, cofounder and CEO of Interchange, a not-for-profit company dedicated to the practice, design, and processes of leadership that allows participatory, interactive learning, and transformation in small and large groups; personal communication, April 28, 2007).

APPRECIATIVE INQUIRY

Change management guru Peter Drucker once said in an interview that "the task of organizational leadership is to create an alignment of strengths that makes a system's weaknesses irrelevant" (cited in Cooperrider & Whitney, 2005, p. xxvii). Appreciative inquiry is a life centric strategy for organizational development and change management designed to do just that, by focusing on the strengths within an organization. This contrasts strikingly with the focus of many management systems and change initiatives, which seems to be fix the problems; the strengths will take care of themselves.

A QUICK COMPARISON

Problem Solving

- o Identify problems
- o Analyze causes

    ○ Analyze possible solutions
    ○ Develop action plans

Metaphor: Organizations are problems to be solved.

Appreciative Inquiry

    ○ Appreciate "What is?" (What gives life?)
    ○ Imagine "What might be?"
    ○ Determine "What should be?"
    ○ Create "What will be?"

Metaphor: Organizations are a mystery to be embraced.

Guiding Assumptions

    ○ In every community, something works.
    ○ What we focus on becomes our reality.
    ○ Reality is created in the moment.
    ○ The act of asking questions influences the community in some way.
    ○ People have more confidence and comfort to journey into the future when they carry forward parts of the past.
    ○ If we carry forward parts of the past, they should be what is best.
    ○ It is important to value differences.
    ○ The language we use creates our reality.

An appreciative inquiry involves four phases. The best ways to organize the activity will change depending on the size of the participating group, but the phases remain the same.

- Discover (appreciating): Articulating strengths and best practices by asking all stakeholders, "What is the best of what is and has been?"
- Dream (envisioning): Envisioning "What might be?" and articulating a results-oriented vision based on the discovered potential and a sense of higher purpose—"What is the world calling us to become?"
- Design (co-constructing): Creating statements that capture the ideal organization and articulating an organization design that people can draw on and magnify the positive core of the organization to realize the dream

- Destiny (sustaining): Identifying how to learn, empower, and adjust/improvise as future unfolds

GETTING STARTED

You can start using appreciative inquiry individually or in small groups. Your list of inquiries may be short and simple or lengthy and complex. To foster a relaxed-alert culture, try using circle or splitting into world café groups so that an environment of trust, confidence, and competence is present. It's important not to hurry through any phase of the inquiry and to work through all four of them on each question. Relying on generative leadership principles, guide the process with meaningful questions that keep everybody focused on common purposes.

Your routine staff meeting can be a starting point. Everyone knows that these meetings can be meaningless and sometimes downright boring. Appreciative inquiry can help you shift from more static and mechanical to more positive and generative staff meetings. One good way to start would be to design questions or scenarios that help your teachers and support staff think deeply and talk about what works well in an area that most needs improvement. You can find useful ideas for both questions and scenarios in *Appreciative Teambuilding: Positive Questions to Bring Out the Best of Your Team* (Whitney, Trosten-Bloom, Cherney, & Fry, 2004).

> Appreciative inquiry can help you shift from more static and mechanical to more positive and generative staff meetings.

Here is one example of a very brief but effective appreciative inquiry with a large number of people. In the plenary session of an industry conference devoted to patient safety in health care, the keynote speaker asked participants to self-organize into groups of 10 or fewer and discuss this question: "When was the last time you experienced excellent service, and what did that feel like?" After 20 minutes of conversation, he asked a second question: "When was the last time you served someone superbly, and what motivated you to do that?" These two simple questions propelled everybody beyond the conventional boundaries of their thinking and conversation, served as a strong foundation for open sharing of knowledge, and helped break through many commonplace presumptions that had blocked effective action (P. Cass, president and CEO of Columbus Medical Association Foundation; personal communication, October 28, 2006).

How would your school team respond to a similar pair of questions about memorable learning experiences? What insights about teamwork could you gain from an appreciative inquiry around the most successful partnership each staff member ever had with someone whose personality and style were very different? Follow-up questions here might include these: How did your differences contribute to everyone's well-being? What strategies did you have for utilizing the differences? "How did your strategy work? What more might you have done to achieve an even more positive outcome?" (Whitney et al., 2004, p. 27). Conversation and facilitation around how this insight can be applied to differences within your own team can contribute to the more generative conversations that you desire and that your staff will appreciate and embrace. You may find your own questions, of course, which adds authenticity to the work.

Please remember that appreciative inquiry is not a quick fix. Questions can lead to generative conversations and action over a long period of time, and your team will self-organize around them if you give up control. In the spirit of the circle and appreciative inquiry, curiosity, community, and positive purpose become the foundation for learning and designing together. Watch natural learning and the living system emerge.

THE U-PROCESS

We think of the U-Process as a social technology for addressing highly complex challenges. It is based on two decades of research by leading experts in generativity, organizational development, and social change, including Peter Senge, Otto Scharmer, Adam Kahane, and Shell Oil Company's renowned Scenario Planning Group. The real-world challenges tackled in the course of this research are very diverse, ranging from the business process change in global companies to the transformation of national governments.

The process involves stages, or activities, that arise from a set of core capacities. Each capacity is a gateway to the next activity. Only as all capacities are developed can a person, group, or community move through the entire process.

The phases, known as "spaces" of the U-Process (see Figure 5.1), represent the activities involved in transformative learning—learning that is deeper and more richly creative than either adaptive or generative learning. It is important here again to understand that this is not a menu of three possible selections, nor are these linear, sequential steps to be completed one after another. Whether one individual or an entire organization is working through a U-Process, these spaces overlap and interact richly during the process.

The Three Spaces

Co-sensing: Transforming perception
   o Observing the current reality carefully and in depth

Co-presencing: Transforming self and will
   o Retreating and reflecting to allow "inner knowing" to emerge

Co-realizing: Transforming action
   o Swift actions in order to bring about the new realities

Capacities

These capacities capture individual and collective abilities needed to discover generative solutions and translate them into effective action. As you develop these, your awareness expands and you begin to "see" the real-world challenges around you in different ways.

- *Suspending:* This involves "seeing beyond the habitual lenses and filters—suspending our mental pictures and concepts, our judgment, our positions, and our expectations about what we will see" (Generon Consulting, 2005, p. 29). Our mental models of reality are not to be ignored or destroyed, but rather, the hidden assumptions embedded in them need to be brought to light and challenged. Leaders invite participants to examine

Figure 5.1

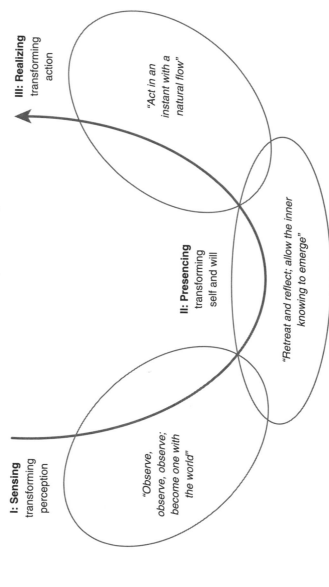

The U-Process Is a Three-Phase Methodology for Addressing Complex Challenges

I: Sensing
transforming perception

"Observe, observe, observe; become one with the world"

II: Presencing
transforming self and will

"Retreat and reflect; allow the inner knowing to emerge"

III: Realizing
transforming action

"Act in an instant with a natural flow"

SOURCE: W. Brian Arthur, Joseph Jaworski, and C. Otto Scharmer

together their current thoughts about processes, issues, or ideas so that everyone can reach a deeper understanding of the current situation. Suspending habits of mind and reflexive judgment allows new connections and emerging patterns in processes, contents, or events to be seen.

- *Redirecting:* The clearer perspective gained by suspending reveals new dimensions of the system and the challenge. Redirecting is the conscious act of shifting attention from the old, habitual way of thinking about a challenge to these new dimensions. Focusing attention on a new reality propels thought toward the points that can bring about change.

- *Letting go and letting come:* New eyes now offer an ability to see from within the source of what emerges. The participants, viewing the current conditions from new perspectives, begin to let go of the old ways and allow for the creation of new beginnings through them. Opportunities for fresh thinking lead toward creative ideas and greater potential expand. The energy for these ideas comes through the individuals and the group as they form together a new sense of the whole.

- *Crystallizing intent:* New ideas are now available to craft new directions. The connectedness of the individuals and ideas is far more apparent and can now bring about a new intent for the organization. New focal points develop, and the group begins the shared process of bringing the intent to a new reality.

- *Rapid prototyping:* A critical point in bringing about new realities involves a rapid response to the new intent. Often, too much time and planning bog down what is a very exciting time. Leaders now trust that the organization (living system) will resolve issues as they arise without the need to overplan or structure the bringing of the ideas forward. "A tenet of prototyping is acting on a concept before that concept is complete or perfect" (Senge, Scharmer, Jaworski, & Flowers, 2004, p. 151).

- *Institutionalizing:* The institutionalizing of the new realities comes through a new sense of connectedness on the part of the individuals, and their own personal realization of their capacities. Coupled with the now-evident external changes and the achievements that result, the ideas, processes, and methods become institutionalized through a new way of being.

  As Adam Kahane says, most change processes are superficial because they don't generate the depth of understanding and commitment that is required for sustaining change in truly demanding circumstances. (Senge et al., 2004, p. 87)

Catalysts for Growth   **6**

Tools and Resources for the Generative School Leader

*Creative solutions often become mired in **adaptive** ways of thinking and dialoguing, resulting in the production of only incremental improvements within the current organizational paradigm. These coping strategies are usually grounded in well-established institutional knowledge or historical traditions and methodologies. The **generative** process requires the acquisition and application of other input fostered through new learning and different perspectives, effectively offering group members new tools for their toolkits in considering alternative possibilities.*

—Tracy Edwards (2007, p. 1)

W e hope by this point that you are inspired and curious about generative leadership and how you can increase your capacity for it. Perhaps you have also discovered some new ideas that will spark the generative journey for you and your school. If so, that is exciting! Here is a collection of personal development tools and facilitation methods that we have compiled to further assist you.

HOW TO USE CHAPTER 6

- The tools are meant to serve as catalysts, not checklists. Consider them points of departure for your own growth and practice. Feel free to adapt, revise, or re-create as you see fit.

- There is no start or end point, nor is there a recommended sequence. Like a craftsman, you'll learn by practice which tool is best suited to your skills and the needs of the moment, and you'll use your best tools over and over again, adapting them as you go.

- No structured templates or step-by-step procedures are given. This is intentional. These tools serve to catalyze and guide growth and change, which you and your school will be undergoing simultaneously.

- Unless noted otherwise, all this material is open-source. This means it is offered for use without charge or control. You are free to modify or adapt the tools as you see fit to suit your needs. We ask, in return, that you keep us informed about the changes you have developed and how they worked in different contexts. (We're still learning, too!)

Suggestions for improvement are also quite welcome.
Send those to us at info@generative-educator.com

Both/And Viewfinder

We have begun with the Both/And Viewfinder because language is both a stepping stone to and a lens on thinking and hidden assumptions. Bringing to mind new language is a simple first lever to apply to new thinking. This is a "visual thinking tool" designed to help you expand "either/or" thinking and language to "both/and," perhaps as you articulate philosophy, vision, expectations, or futures. Using the chart as a springboard may help you transform more traditional, mechanistic language into more generative language. The tool is a suggestion. Use your own language if ours is not appropriate for your context. Notice that the arrows in Figure 6.1 point outward from the second circle, hinting at still further possibilities that you (or we) may discover.

Using This Tool

- The both/and chart gives the generative leader a visual that can be used for conversations, planning, moving "from-to" . . . getting tough problems unstuck. It can be used as a handout at staff development sessions or for dialogue with school improvement teams, focus points in process group sessions, or simply as a tool for personal development.

Figure 6.1

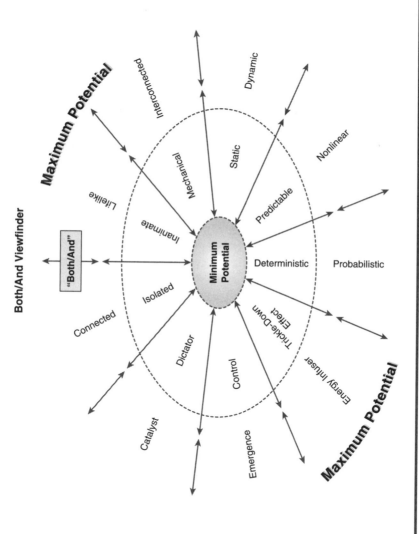

Unpacking the Six Hallmarks

Developing the six hallmarks (see Chapter 4 and Figure 6.2) is a lifelong practice. Here are a number of ideas for conscious action that can strengthen your development as a generative leader. Consider them as entry points through which you can determine comfortable and clear actions that enhance your growth as a leader.

Using This Tool

- *Choose one.* Find a hallmark that is an engaging and comfortable starting step for you and that you would be willing to practice for a period of time, perhaps a month or so.

- *Be observant.* Watch yourself as you develop the hallmark. What internal and external changes do you observe? How do you feel? Can you see differences in others' responses to you? Do you interact with others differently—more meaningfully, more creatively, more openly, and more inclusively? Are you feeling less uncomfortable as you become more adept at the new behavior or process? What works best for you? What other questions help focus your self-monitoring?

- *Talk to a colleague.* Sometimes talking is the best way to listen to your thoughts and to find the real and meaningful roads for your journey. Hearing yourself think can provide fascinating and meaningful personal insight.

- *As you become comfortable with one hallmark, add more.* Not too many at once, and take your time. Generativity won't be built in a day. The important thing is to begin and to build your awareness of your thinking and behavior.

- *Celebrate occasionally.* Give yourself a good pat on the back—or better yet, a dinner out—or some gift for making changes. You're worth it!

Figure 6.2

The Six Hallmarks

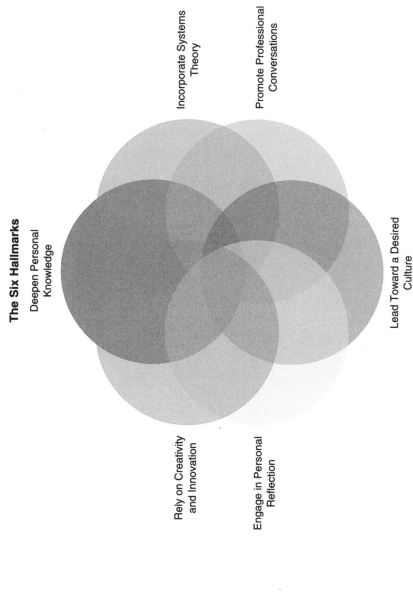

Deepen Personal
Knowledge

Incorporate Systems
Theory

Promote Professional
Conversations

Lead Toward a Desired
Culture

Engage in Personal
Reflection

Rely on Creativity
and Innovation

Hallmark 1: Deepen Personal Knowledge

Generative leaders bring rich knowledge to the conversation to inform, direct, and give context to everybody's thinking. They are avid continual learners who go well beyond the bounds of administration and education in search of new ideas and understanding.

Stepping Beyond Your Boundaries

Read, read, read! There are many excellent journals, books, and Web sites on topics ranging from classroom management to budgets. Choose carefully to ensure a wide spectrum of sources that offer varying viewpoints. Look outside the realm of education for insights that may help you discern unifying concepts hidden by the busyness and clutter of your own day-to-day world.

Go! Attend seminars and conferences whenever possible. Seek new knowledge and fresh perspectives rather than instruction on problem-solving approaches. Take a partner with you to better digest and interpret the presentations heard. Creative insights and approaches are easier to discover when your range of experience and stimulus is widened beyond your immediate circumstances.

Convene! Take the lead. Invite a small cadre of fellow leaders to your school or district. Select a simple, important question that you can engage in candid and meaningful conversation.

Hunt! Seek out others who are experts in various fields and contact them. An e-mail or telephone call from a professional seeking new knowledge is never out of bounds. Know, too, that such exchanges are never one-way: Your inquiry is a gift that will benefit the other professional's growth as well.

Step out! Look outside the field of education for ideas that might open your thinking a bit. How would you import a process or strategy from one professional arena into your own? What are the analogous elements in your world? Look for innovative approaches. For example, how do the challenges facing other caring professions, such as health care, resemble the ones you face? What approaches have helped hospitals deal with these challenges and improve their performance? The business section at your favorite bookstore would be an excellent place to start. What other sections of the bookstore might you explore?

Express yourself! Talk with others who can inform your thinking. Have the courage to let them probe your logic and even your vocabulary. Discover your own hidden assumptions and refine your understanding.

Invite! Welcome diverse ideas, those that will challenge your commonsense assumptions. Explore them like an intriguing puzzle, seeking to understand their basis and their meaning to the people who hold them. Your sincere desire to understand is essential to building the trust needed for authentic conversation.

Hallmark 2: Blend Living Systems Theory With Practice

Leadership based on living systems principles looks, sounds, and feels quite different from the traditional approach found in most schools. It challenges us to release control at the same time that we hold on to our authority. Generative leaders look for creative ideas within the context of living systems.

Stepping Beyond Your Boundaries

Dig a bit. Explore systems and complexity theories. Chapter 2 introduced some of the basic information on living systems. Some of the leaders that have researched and written on this include Peter Senge, Meg Wheatley, Joseph Jaworski, and Sam Crowell. A deeper shared understanding of living systems, developed through conversation in your school/district, will begin the shift toward a renewed spirit and direction for everyone.

Question. Participants in a generative environment always question the status quo. They share a passion for continual learning and improvement. They embrace growth and change even though it is sometimes difficult.

Anchor your intent. Know that your vision and intent are the hubs around which your school lives. Holding fast to this vision and intent will cause the living system to respond to your energy.

Include. It is all about bringing others into the conversation. The conversations that you facilitate within the living system will translate into new energies that bring about the desired culture—that is, assuming that there is action taken at some point following the conversations!

Hallmark 3: Promote Professional Conversations

Conversation is one of the major carriers of the information that nourishes a living system. Since it affects the relationships of the system so strongly (positively or negatively), it is arguably the most important carrier. Every person in your school affects the system through each of their conversations.

Conversations give you an opportunity to think out loud—a valuable and necessary part of creative decision making. Strategic conversations, designed to take thinking and planning into the future, are primary planning tools for generative leaders.

Stepping Beyond Your Boundaries

Talk productively. It is always fascinating to monitor the discussions happening during the informal times of the day. Each conversation affects the potential future of the school. Maximize them by being as positive and insightful as possible.

Listen. Really listen—with all your senses and full awareness. Listen without judging and without a hidden agenda. As others share their ideas with you, openly take in their words and ask questions that lead to a deeper understanding of what they have in mind.

Gather information. As you gather information on any topic or idea, it is important to look closely at the source and consider its validity and compatibility with your situation. Ask yourself, "Who or what is informing you?"

Develop relationships. Be authentic. You will find that the valued conversations that permeate the environment will translate to better understandings of each other.

Trust good feedback. Honest feedback is a precious commodity. The tough part is trusting the input to the point that you adjust your thinking and actions. Certainly, your filters will need to be active when considering any feedback, but be sure to look within the feedback for nuggets of powerful insight.

Trust yourself. Your values, intuition, and intellect can determine the weight you put on others' perspectives and ideas. Take what you believe is of value.

Hallmark 4: Engage in Personal Reflection

Generative leaders know the value of taking time to think, write, listen to music, paint, walk, create. It means taking time each day to fully integrate the fresh and unique thinking of both yourself and others and give it your own quiet interpretation. Allow time for the frenzy of the world to subside so that you can best discern the more subtle meanings and linkages within your world.

Stepping Beyond Your Boundaries

Think. This might seem obvious, but thinking should not be confused with doing or acting. If you access your ability to really think, you will probably discover how much you don't think in many other circumstances. Busy lives can produce automated behaviors.

Listen. Listen to yourself. See if you can connect with the ways in which you are processing new information. Open your awareness of your mental processing as you are in a reflective state.

Breathe and observe. Ever notice the calming effect a deep breath has? Start to use this intentionally to center your mental focus, to help discard unwanted energies from your day and produce a greater sensitivity for clear thought. As you do this more often, you'll notice a heightened ability to observe the world more keenly.

Be alone. Consider locating a place in your home, neighborhood, or workplace that can be designated as your "serenity zone" and attempt to keep that space for your reflective rituals. Or make a walk, bike ride, boat ride, or even a regular visit to a welcoming shade tree part of your daily pattern.

Write. Create a notebook or journal that can act as an outlet for your deep thoughts. Much like good conversation with others, you can surprise yourself with what you really think by actually putting it in writing.

Hallmark 5: Lead Toward a Desired Culture

This hallmark is the essence of generativity. Knowing vividly what you want to lead *toward* will give intent and energy to your dream. Invite others to participate in the conversations that will develop scenarios and add diversity and fresh ideas to your thoughts. Give full reign to the possibility that what your team produces may actually be more than you thought possible. What you imagine and design together will surpass what you ever thought could be in the "old system."

Stepping Beyond Your Boundaries

Imagine. The ability to imagine new futures for today's schools is a crucial trait of the generative leader. Envision the best and live toward it.

Be proactive, not reactive. Good leaders initiate direction. Capture the generative ideas and follow through.

Commit to action. Bring the best ideas to life through good planning, clear articulation of actions, and verification of outcomes.

Invite opinions. Invite others to participate in the co-envisioning of the desired culture. Their ideas and passion are essential. Diverse thinking feeds creativity.

Hallmark 6: Rely on Creativity and Innovation

Generative leadership is about being creative. There is no way around it. Direct as much energy as possible toward being imaginative, innovative—and courageous. Give yourself permission to take risks, look for new and novel ideas, and try new ways of solving problems. Discover your own creativity. Crossing personal boundaries is a part of the call to order for the best schools conceivable.

Stepping Beyond Your Boundaries

Become playful. As new ideas emerge, toss them around in fun, easygoing ways. In a relaxed state, your brain taps into its more creative regions, and wonderful new ideas become increasingly sophisticated. Watch where the conversations lead!

Mindmap. Access your natural, visual abilities by having a large white board or sheets of butcher paper available while you are "playing." Be sure to have colorful markers and maybe even put some fun music on as a backdrop. The caliber of your idea generation will increase and the spirit of the activity will soon flow into all the learning spaces of the school. Even if the purpose of the discussion is to solve a tough problem, rely on these creative elements to improve the eventual outcome.

Conquer the "judging" mind. The ability to be self-critical is a strength. Too much of it can obstruct positive forward movement. Conquer the tendency to "not do" because of an overly sensitive "judging" mind. Your creativity will bloom as you become willing to follow, to give an idea a try.

Listen to the "what if" mind. "Perhaps there is another way." "What if this project was approached from this angle?" "Have we considered other opinions on this before we take actions?" Generative thinkers and leaders cherish the world that can become.

The Modality Matrix

Information fuels the living system. The leadership modalities introduced in Chapter 4 are an excellent framework within which to examine the state of individual and collective relationships inside your system. They help each leader examine his or her own leadership tendencies and consider the factors that give rise to them. The Modality Matrix (Figures 6.3a and 6.3b) links the individual modalities with group modalities by including the persons, methods, process, and environments with which one works. Plotting your evaluation of both dimensions lets you see your school's current degree of generativity.

Using This Tool

- Two versions of the Modality Matrix are provided here. The first one has all the visual symbols clearly identified in Figure 6.3a. This version can be used for presentations to teachers, administrators, school boards, or student leadership groups.

- The Modality Matrix in Figure 6.3b is intended as a template for your own work. Use it for periodic individual reflection and as a tool for group conversations. The fainter visual symbols are intended to make it easy for you to record your own ideas or capture the trajectory of a conversation.

- What is "stuck" in your school? How would you describe the relationships between the elements in your system that are "stuck"? Examine other system elements, such as hiring processes or teaching methods. What are they like most of the time? Where would you place them on the matrix?

- Consider using the operational indicators to prompt discussion addressed in Chapter 4. How can they help initiate good conversation about the new futures possible in your school? For example, Indicator 2 suggests, "Everyone in the school is empowered to participate in the school's progress." Layer that onto the matrix to explore the relevance of that condition in the school. From your perspective, is that a procedure? A process? Is there any conversation that would suggest this is "stuck" in your school? (See Chapter 4 for the complete list of operational indicators.)

94

Figure 6.3a

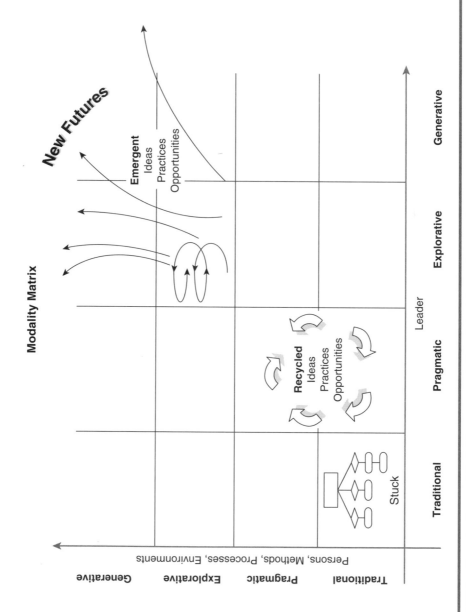

Modality Matrix

New Futures

Emergent
Ideas
Practices
Opportunities

Recycled
Ideas
Practices
Opportunities

Stuck

Leader

Traditional　　Pragmatic　　Explorative　　Generative

Persons, Methods, Processes, Environments

Traditional　Pragmatic　Explorative　Generative

Figure 6.3b

Modality Matrix

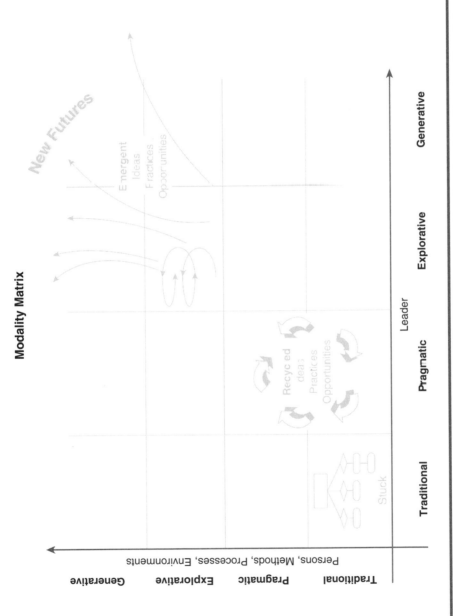

Critical Visioning Web and Waterfall

"Having a vision" for your school or district is terminology that is relatively common throughout our educational infrastructure. Most educators have been through some type of planning activity in which the long-range direction of the school is discussed and a "vision statement" is written, published, and posted. All too often, these exercises are perfunctory, producing results that offer little invigoration or meaningful direction.

The Critical Visioning Web presented here may look on the surface like one of the traditional planning models you have seen before, but it is not. It was developed by leaders of the Automotive Multimedia Interface Collaboration (AMI-C) to tackle the challenge of unifying 12 global vehicle manufacturers for a common purpose—a purpose they needed to define together, despite their tremendous differences in culture, organization, and technology. It has since been adopted as the primary planning framework by the Convergence Education Foundation and used to help many schools become more generative. It is one small example of how generative leaders can very effectively transpose fundamental principles from one working domain to another very different one.

What else makes this tool different? The questions embedded in it. These are generative questions. They may look simple, but they can lead to incisive examination of commonplace assumptions and things taken for granted. They are also appreciative questions, leading participants to focus on the strengths on which they can build rather than on deficits.

Generative leadership of the planning process is key to making this happen most effectively: Do the environment and context allow participants to work in a relaxed alert state? Does the experience provide complex sensory experience and foster active processing? Are constructive relationships fostered, and does information flow freely from outside and within the system? If these conditions are well satisfied, then this sequence of questions will lead to very effective outcomes.

The term *critical vision* signals some important things. A critical vision is one that points toward a new future and links this to the participants' values and beliefs. It is the answer to the question *"What future 'state' do we want to create?"* It expresses a long-range destination and invites everyone to envision and work toward this. It becomes the opportunity to ask frequently, "Are we there yet?" and "Is there another way we can get there?" We are calling it a "critical" vision statement to capture the sense of urgency that needs to be present.

Using This Tool

- Two versions of the tool are offered for your use. The first, Figure 6.4a, reflects how a critical vision and mission might look if leaders functioned in an explorative/generative environment. Figure 6.4b presents the same flow of questions in a more linear fashion. Either tool is appropriated for use as school leaders work toward the shared commitment to the vision and mission of the school.

- The first two questions are designed to catalyze envision ing and the development of the identity that animates the living system that is your school or district. These are the critical cornerstones for all the other stages and will carry forward as the vital guiding threads to the everyday work of living this plan—so invest in them well!

- The shift to action begins with strategic objectives, which emerge from asking the third essential question, *"What are we really trying to accomplish?"* Read this question again, placing emphasis on the word *really*. This invitation to dig deep and expand the horizon of collective thinking will help you uncover hidden assumptions and break down habitual status quo thinking. From this conversation, new strategic objectives will be born, offering a new sense of direction and possibility.

- Essential Question 4 brings you to your deliverables. Your deliverables are what come from your strategic objectives and are the result of this question, *"How do we effectively meet our objectives?"* Again, we would ask you to emphasize the word *effectively*. If your deliverables aren't going to be effective, why select them? If your processes for achieving the deliverables aren't very effective, why not improve them?

- Project definitions should emerge from deliverables, so the fifth essential question is, *"What do we actually (currently) do?"* This question always produces amazement, as people throughout the organization discover activities and events they were unaware of before. Valuable learning occurs as people realize how simplistic their mental models of the organization have been and how many untested presumptions were embedded within them.

- The fine details of daily work are generated by the final stage of the critical visioning process. Project plans contain the detailed decisions and activities that make up daily life for everyone within the learning environment and community. The question *"How do we execute?"* prompts everyone to focus on actions, budgets, milestones, efficiency, and communications. It also brings to life the question, *"How will we come together to do this?"* What principles or agreements will we all commit to as we work toward our critical vision?

The Critical Visioning Process

Vision Statement

Essential Question 1: "What future state do we *want* to create?"

Mission Statement

Essential Question 2: "What is our *unique* reason for being?"

Strategic Objectives

Essential Question 3: "What are we *really* trying to accomplish?"

Deliverables

Essential Question 4: "How do we *effectively* meet our objectives?"

Project Definitions

Essential Question 5: "What do we *actually* (currently) do?"

Project Plans

Essential Question 6: "How do we *execute?*"

Figure 6.4a

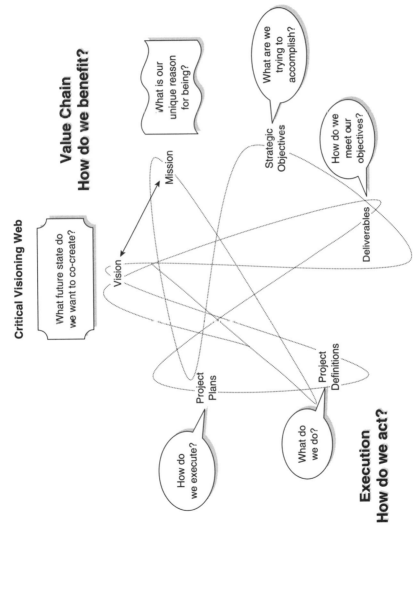

Critical Visioning Web

Value Chain
How do we benefit?

What is our unique reason for being?

What are we trying to accomplish?

How do we meet our objectives?

Mission

Strategic Objectives

Vision

Deliverables

What future state do we want to co-create?

Project Plans

Project Definitions

How do we execute?

What do we do?

Execution
How do we act?

SOURCE: Adapted with permission. D. Acton & S. McCormick (personal communication, April 2003)

Figure 6.4b

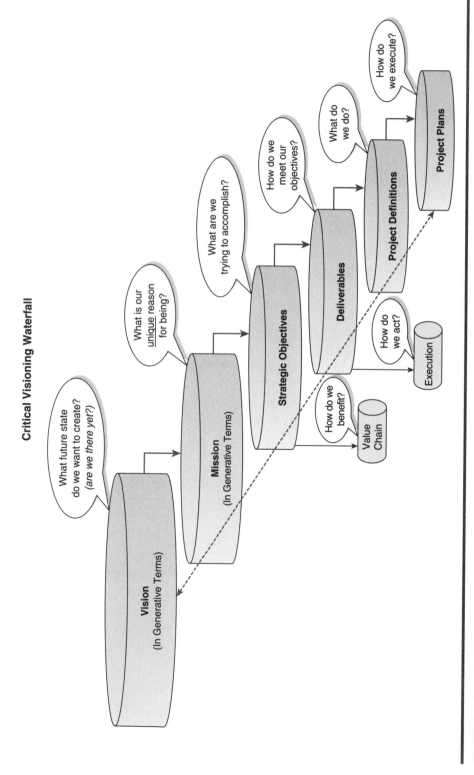

Critical Visioning Waterfall

SOURCE: Adapted with permission. D. Acton & S. McCormick (personal communication, April 2003)

The Brain Learning Cycle

The Brain Learning Cycle presented here is an adaptation of Dr. James Zull's natural learning model (see Chapter 3) to the needs of K–12 classroom educators.

Using This Tool

The Brain Learning Cycle (Figure 6.5) is a chart for checking your use of the four stages of natural learning. A good planning document for staff meetings, professional development, and teacher observation, it can also be used for lesson planning.

- Use the four sections of the chart to be sure that you are including the natural progression of experience to action.

- Be sure that you give adults (or students) an initial experience that is engaging and that provides an emotional connection for learning.

- Allow time for connections to prior knowledge, planning/ designing/creating, and demonstrating or presenting knowledge, plans, designs, and so on.

- For more in-depth work, your participants will go around and through the circle many times.

- The line intersecting the circle indicates that concrete experience and active testing are observable behaviors. You can see them *outside* as the learner processes. Reflective observation and abstract hypotheses tend to happen quietly, or *inside,* as the learner processes.

Following is one way to use the Brain Learning Cycle for designing a staff meeting followed by designing/planning:

1. Begin the meeting with a **concrete experience.** This might be a demonstration, a story, a small group discussion, or a short article for reading or jigsawing followed by dialogue in small groups.

Figure 6.5

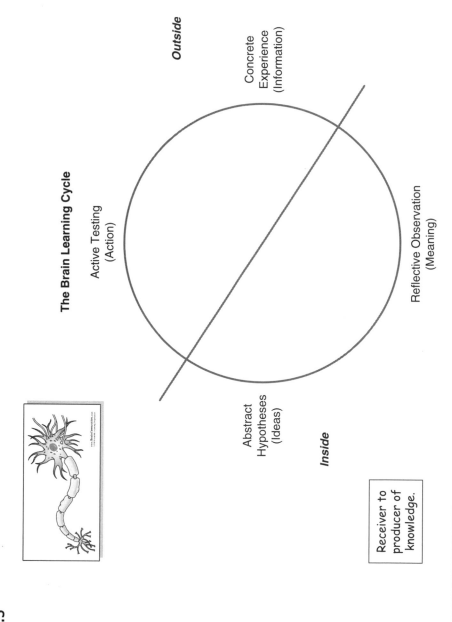

The Brain Learning Cycle

Outside

Active Testing
(Action)

Concrete
Experience
(Information)

Reflective Observation
(Meaning)

Abstract
Hypotheses
(Ideas)

Inside

Receiver to
producer of
knowledge.

SOURCE: From Zull, J. E. (2002). *The Art of Changing the Brain: Enriching Teaching by Exploring the Biology of Learning.* Copyright © James E. Zull. Published by Stylus Publishing, LLC. Reprinted with permission of the author.

2. Allow time for **reflection and integration** of prior knowledge. Questions that lead to reflection might include the following: "What connections are you making to your thinking and/or practice?" "What does this mean for you?" "Where have you seen or done this before? What is similar or different for you?"

3. Encourage the staff to generate new ideas or make new hypotheses from the integration of the information. This is **abstract hypothesis.** You might ask the following: "What ideas does this information help you generate?" "What might you do next?" "What is your hypothesis about this situation or the possibility of new perspectives and action?" "What plans might you design from this information/experience?"

4. Take action and **actively test** new ideas and/or hypotheses. Explain ideas and present them to others, write a futures story about the new ideas, embed ideas in school improvement plans, design new environments and/or instructional approaches, assess new processes, both quantitatively and qualitatively.

The brain perceives and acts naturally. Experiencing, reflecting and integrating, hypothesizing, and actively testing appear to be cumulative and iterative. Remember that they do not happen in a linear fashion. Your staff will tend to self-organize around the experiences and ideas if they are emotionally involved in a positive way with the initiative and find it meaningful. Expect active involvement and good questions, and expect to be involved yourself as part of the process. *Your staff will naturally become producers rather than simply receivers of knowledge.* This gives you the perfect opportunity to influence rather than control—and to use your authority to set a deadline!

Brain/Mind Principles and Capacities Wheels

Ingredients for Effective Conversations

Rich conversations enhance the capacities of all who participate in them. With a focus on natural learning at the core, educators at all levels can deeply explore how learning is occurring in
the classroom, with individual students, and most important, with
themselves. As outlined in Chapter 3, environments that create a
relaxed and alert state, involve learning that is immersed in complex experiences, and include active processing of those experiences as a priority bring greater potential for each individual to
discover and learn. The 12 Brain/Mind Principles and Capacities
(as developed by Renate and Geoffrey Caine) are graphically rep-
resented here (see Figures 6.6 and 6.7), with the three interactive elements at the bottom of each wheel.

Using This Tool

- Consider using the capacities as conversation points
  when exploring the learning environments established in
  your school. For example, are the students being given
  opportunities to "engage their capacity to recognize and
  master essential patterns"? Are the teachers aware of
  the need to "engage both their ability to focus on attention and learn from the peripheral context"?

- Each capacity brings opportunity to professionally and legitimately question the current status of the learning, working, and leading environments.

- Informing parents about natural learning processes
  brings additional health to the living system. The capacities and principles offer information points to help parents
  better understand the ways we all learn. Incorporating
  pertinent information in newsletters, at open house
  events, during informal conversations, and even in discussions with students can bring valuable information to
  members of the school community.

- Reproduce the wheels and use them as tools to begin
  conversations at staff meetings. What are we noticing in
  our school?

Figure 6.6

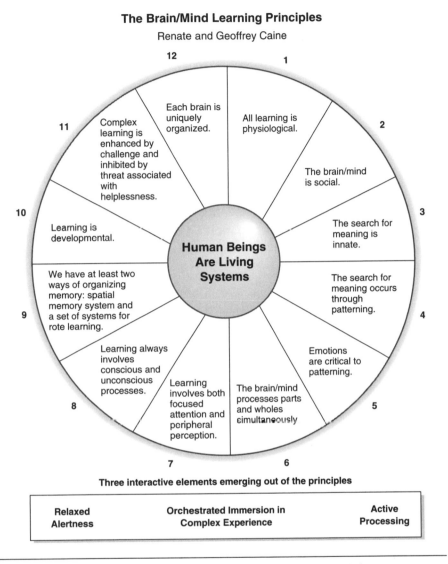

The Brain/Mind Learning Principles
Renate and Geoffrey Caine

- 12 — Each brain is uniquely organized.
- 1 — All learning is physiological.
- 11 — Complex learning is enhanced by challenge and inhibited by threat associated with helplessness.
- 2 — The brain/mind is social.
- 10 — Learning is developmental.
- 3 — The search for meaning is innate.
- 9 — We have at least two ways of organizing memory: spatial memory system and a set of systems for rote learning.
- 4 — The search for meaning occurs through patterning.
- 8 — Learning always involves conscious and unconscious processes.
- 5 — Emotions are critical to patterning.
- 7 — Learning involves both focused attention and peripheral perception.
- 6 — The brain/mind processes parts and wholes simultaneously

Center: **Human Beings Are Living Systems**

Three interactive elements emerging out of the principles

Relaxed Alertness	Orchestrated Immersion in Complex Experience	Active Processing

SOURCE: Caine, R. N., Caine, G., McClintic, C., & Klimek, K. (2004)

- An excellent resource created explicitly for use as a field book for educators is *12 Brain/Mind Learning Principles in Action* by Caine, Caine, McClintic, and Klimek published by Corwin Press in 2004, with a second edition to be released in 2008. Many valuable ideas and in-depth actions, supported by this research, are outlined there.

Figure 6.7

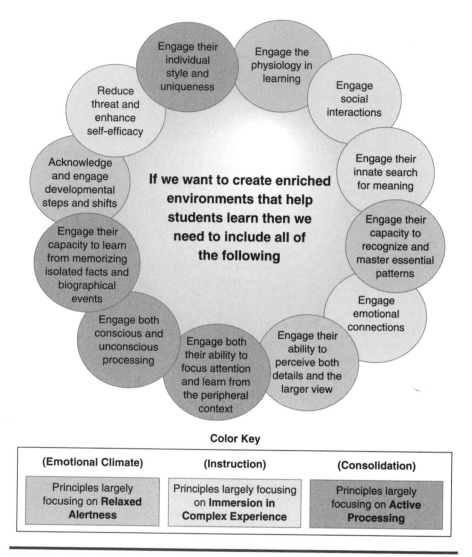

Engage their individual style and uniqueness

Engage the physiology in learning

Engage social interactions

Reduce threat and enhance self-efficacy

Acknowledge and engage developmental steps and shifts

Engage their innate search for meaning

If we want to create enriched environments that help students learn then we need to include all of the following

Engage their capacity to recognize and master essential patterns

Engage their capacity to learn from memorizing isolated facts and biographical events

Engage emotional connections

Engage both conscious and unconscious processing

Engage both their ability to focus attention and learn from the peripheral context

Engage their ability to perceive both details and the larger view

Color Key

(Emotional Climate)	(Instruction)	(Consolidation)
Principles largely focusing on **Relaxed Alertness**	Principles largely focusing on **Immersion in Complex Experience**	Principles largely focusing on **Active Processing**

SOURCE: Caine, R. N., Caine, G., McClintic, C., & Klimek, K. (2004)

Generativity, Living Systems, and Brain/Mind Learning: The Processes and Procedures Lens

Generative leaders begin to see all aspects of their work through new eyes. The language of generative leaders helps guide the conversations and actions in alignment with the blended intertwinement of generativity, living systems, and brain/mind learning.

The Processes and Procedures Lens (Figure 6.8) is a visual tool to consider the relationship between various aspects of the school and the surrounding system, weaving those specific aspects through the lens of the generative leader, then continuing to engage in those conversations and actions as the circular image represents.

Using This Tool

- This is a visual connection tool that demonstrates connections between typical school processes and the foundational elements of generative school leadership that we have developed.

- The arrows invite you to continually assess the status of the three elements within your school procedures: (1) to observe and question; (2) to reflect, develop, and act; and finally, (3) to assess.

- This may be a visual tool for staff development, to introduce the three foundational elements and to help focus conversations.

- It is also a tool for personal development through the six hallmarks.

Figure 6.8

Processes and Procedures Lens

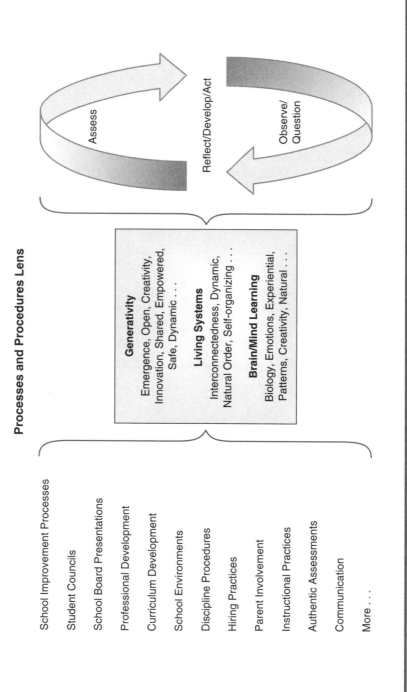

School Improvement Processes

Student Councils

School Board Presentations

Professional Development

Curriculum Development

School Environments

Discipline Procedures

Hiring Practices

Parent Involvement

Instructional Practices

Authentic Assessments

Communication

More . . . .

Assess

Reflect/Develop/Act

Observe/
Question

Generativity
Emergence, Open, Creativity,
Innovation, Shared, Empowered,
Safe, Dynamic . . . .

Living Systems
Interconnectedness, Dynamic,
Natural Order, Self-organizing . . .

Brain/Mind Learning
Biology, Emotions, Experiential,
Patterns, Creativity, Natural . . .

108

From the Authors' Bookshelves

We are all avid readers, and we each have a large library of favorite books. Many of these had a significant influence on this book but did not rise to the level of being cited in the text. We each list a few of our favorites below, along with a thumbnail description conveying what we most appreciate about each one. We hope you enjoy them, and benefit from reading them, as much as we have!

Karl J. Klimek

How to Think Like Leonardo da Vinci: Seven Steps to Genius Every Day

Michael J. Gelb, Bantam Dell, 1998.

Learning about the Renaissance has become a fascination for me. Art, music, and creativity were the core elements around which life was focused. Gelb takes a close look at Leonardo and builds on his seven principles: Curiositsa, Dimonstrazione, Sensazione, Sfumato, Arte/Scienza, Corporalita, and Connessione. More wonderful points around which to personally grow and develop

Solving Tough Problems: An Open Way of Talking, Listening, and Creating New Realities.

Adam Kahane, Berrett-Kohler Publishers, 2004.

The opportunity to work with Adam and his team from Generon Consulting was an experience that opened new eyes for me. The global work being done through their efforts provides me strength, because the answers needed to solve tough problems with schools are discoverable. Seemingly unsolvable problems found direction and success through the efforts of Adam and his colleagues. Generative principles are at the core.

Nuts! Southwest Airlines' Crazy Recipe for Business and Personal Success

Kevin L. Freiberg and Jacqueline A. Freiberg, Bard Press, 1996.

An organizational eye-opener for me, this book introduced me to the "big picture" of a successful organization that was not education based. Creativity, courage, pattern breaking, and tenacity combine to redefine and challenge the legacy airlines.

Go Vertical! Life Has No Ceiling

Richard J. "Rico" Racosky, Rocketfuel Publishing, 2003.

In the early days of 1990, Rico crossed my path, and his *"dreams + action = Reality"* formula for living entered my world and belief system. Since then, our friendship has resulted in numerous collaborative efforts to benefit kids and adults alike. Using the story of the Wright Brothers, his formula triggers thinking through perspectives that give readers a greater will to follow their passion. Consider what Orville and Wilbur accomplished without the modern technologies and luxuries we have today. Even without, they changed the world forever.

Pour Your Heart Into It: How Starbucks Built a Company One Cup at a Time

Howard Schultz and Dori Jones Yang, Hyperion Publishers, 1997.

Those close to me know that I like my Starbucks coffee. During a stop for a cup near Jackson, Michigan, a passionate employee turned me on to this book about the philosophies and goals of this highly successful organization. Attention to detail cannot be overlooked. Their organizational ingredients provide great flavor for conversation!

Elsie Ritzenhein

Leadership Is an Art

Max DePree, Dell Publishing, 1989.

Max DePree was the chief executive officer of Herman Miller, Inc., when he wrote this book. His authenticity, honesty, and prose are engaging. I have read several of DePree's books, but this is my favorite. And he leaves room in the margins to write notes.

Jamming: The Art and Discipline of Business Creativity

John Kao, HarperBusiness, 1996.

Kao's intent to bring creativity to the forefront of the manager's attention, and practice comes from his other life as a jazz pianist. Using jazz improvisation as the metaphor for creativity in business, Kao brings a fresh, exciting perspective to thinking about leadership. This book helped me begin the generative journey, even though I didn't know it then. After many reads, his ideas continue to be unique and inviting.

Learning as a Way of Being: Strategies for Survival in a World of Permanent White Water

Peter B. Vaill, Jossey-Bass Publishers, 1996.

This is another of my early reads on leadership that influenced my road toward generativity. Thanks to my friend Sam Crowell for suggesting Vaill's excellent writing about the world of "permanent white water" and the changes in thinking for managerial leaders that are essential in this context. We have been experiencing a permanent white water in education for some time, and Vaill's insights are more valuable than ever for me. I encourage you to take a look if this book isn't already on your shelf.

The Creative Habit: Learn It and Use It for Life

Twyla Tharp, Simon & Schuster, 2003.

"Creativity is not a gift from the gods," says dancer and choreographer Tharp. "It is the product of preparation and effort, and it's within reach of everyone who wants to achieve it." Creativity is the essence of generative leadership, and Tharp provides an interesting, meaningful, and pleasant entry into creative thinking and practice. Her stories about personal experiences and exercises for practicing creativity are useful and pertinent. If this type of thinking is new for you, Tharp takes you gently to the edge and encourages you to take the leap. It's worth the risk.

A Whole New Mind: Why Right-Brainers Will Rule the Future

Daniel H. Pink, Penguin Group, 2005.

Pink takes the reader to the world of fMRIs, abundance, Asia, and automation through R-Directed Thinking and L-Directed Thinking. I thoroughly enjoyed this easy read about what he describes as the six senses: design, story, symphony, empathy, play, and meaning, all of which he believes are essential in a high-concept, high-touch, and conceptual age. He brings us to creative thinking from a different perspective—one that is current, critical, and insightful. The book is enjoyable and easy to follow. Pink quotes Twyla Tharp, which makes this another of my valuable connective resources. *A Whole New Mind* is a must-read for generative leaders.

Kathryn D. Sullivan

Orbiting the Giant Hairball: A Corporate Fool's Guide to Surviving With Grace

Gordon MacKenzie, Viking Press, 1998.

I love this book! McKenzie spent 30 years at Hallmark Cards, rising from sketch artist to middle manager before creating for himself the niche of "creative paradox"—anybody who can sell that job title to a large company is certainly creative! He gets at the crux of the universal challenge: how to support essential living processes such as creativity and learning in social structures that prefer machinelike order and predictability. His fabulous mix of doodles, sketches, fonts, and paintings are good medicine for a fallen-away scientist/engineer!

Leading Minds

Howard Gardner (with Emma Laskin), Basic Books, 1995.

A fascinating book that looks at how the mind of the leader and the minds of the followers determine leadership approaches and affect outcomes. Gardner highlights the strong link between traditional creators (artists and scientist) and leaders in politics, business, and the military; shows the pivotal role played by mental models; and reminds us of the importance of story. The 11 renowned leaders he uses as his prisms include J. Robert Oppenheimer (father of the atom bomb), Martin Luther King, Jr., Pope John XXII, Margaret Mead, Margaret Thatcher, George C. Marshall, and Eleanor Roosevelt.

The Happiness Hypothesis: Finding Modern Truth in Ancient Wisdom

Jonathan Haidt, Basic Books, 2006.

Life and literature have taught me that no matter who we are or where we live, there are a few key lessons we're here to learn, and they will come at us over and over again in many different forms. Haidt reached a similar conclusion from his work as a social psychologist and teacher: Ten "great ideas" have been discovered by several of the world's civilizations and are often expressed in remarkably similar terms. He traces these roots, looks at the new questions raised by modern science, and extracts lessons that still apply to modern life.

Thinkertoys: A Handbook of Creative-Thinking Techniques

Michael Michalko, Ten Speed Press, 2006.

A toy chest for your mind! Michalko is a creativity expert who works with Fortune 500 companies and government agencies worldwide. Thinkertoys contains a variety of fun tips, tools, and exercises that catalyze individual and group creative thinking. Lots of "Aha!" moments in this volume.

The Courage to Teach

Parker Palmer, Jossey-Bass Publishers, 1999.

One of the most eloquent and moving books I've ever read about teaching (which is leading) and the inner journey needed to be a good teacher. Palmer probes the universal yet personal questions at the heart of teaching and leading—the great mystery of the human self, how to be humble and confident at the same time, how and why we risk the human connections that are essential to life and love and teaching. His writing is both rigorous and eloquent, both passionate and precise.

Resources

Briggs, J., & Peat, F. D. (1999). *Seven life lessons of chaos: Spiritual wisdom from the science of change.* New York: HarperCollins.

Brooks, J. G., & Brooks, M. G. (1999). *In search of understanding: The case for constructivist classrooms.* Alexandria, VA: Association for Supervision and Curriculum Development.

Brown, J. L., & Moffett, C. A. (1999). *The hero's journey: How educators can transform schools and improve learning.* Alexandria, VA: Association for Supervision and Curriculum Development.

Caine, G., Caine, R. N., & Crowell, S. (1999). *MindShifts: A brain-compatible process for professional development and the renewal of education.* Tucson, AZ: Zephyr Press.

Clark, E. T., Jr. (1997). *Designing & implementing an integrated curriculum: A student-centered approach.* Brandon, VT: Holistic Education Press.

Crowell, S., Caine, R., & Caine, G. (1998). *The re-enchantment of learning: A manual for teacher renewal and classroom transformation.* Thousand Oaks, CA: Corwin Press.

DePree, M. (1989). *Leadership is an art.* New York: Dell.

DePree, M. (1992). *Leadership jazz.* New York: Dell.

Dickmann, M. H., & Stanford-Blair, N. (2002). *Connecting leadership to the brain.* Thousand Oaks, CA: Corwin Press.

Ellinor, L., & Gerard, G. (1998). *Dialogue.* New York: John Wiley.

Freiberg, K. L., & Freiberg, J. A. (1996). *Nuts! Southwest Airlines' crazy recipe for business and personal success.* Austin, TX: Bard Press.

Fullan, M. (1993). *Change forces: Probing the depths of educational reform.* London: Falmer Press.

Fullan, M. (2000). *The Jossey-Bass reader on educational leadership.* San Francisco: Jossey-Bass.

Gardner, H. (with E. Laskin). (1995). *Learning minds.* New York: Basic Books.

Gelb, M. (1998). *How to think like Leonardo daVinci: Seven steps to genius every day.* New York: Bantam Dell.

Gergen, K. J. (1994). *Toward transformation in social knowledge.* Thousand Oaks, CA: Sage.

Goldberg, E. (2001). *The executive brain: Frontal lobes and the civilized mind.* Oxford, UK: Oxford University Press.

Goleman, D. (1998). *Working with emotional intelligence.* New York: Bantam.

Goleman, D., Kaufman, P., & Ray, M. (1992). *The creative spirit.* New York: Penguin Books.

Gryskiewicz, S. S. (1999). *Positive turbulence: Developing climates for creativity, innovation, and renewal.* San Francisco: Jossey-Bass.

James, J. (1996). *Thinking in the future tense: Leadership skills for a new age.* New York: Simon & Schuster.

Jaworski, J. (1998). *Synchronicity: The inner path of leadership.* San Francisco: Berrett-Koehler.

Johansson, F. (2006). *The Medici effect: What elephants and epidemics can teach us about innovation.* Boston: Harvard Business School Press.

Kahane, A. (2004). *Solving tough problems: An open way of talking, listening, and creating new realities.* San Francisco: Berrett-Koehler.

Kao, J. (1996). *Jamming: The art and discipline of business creativity.* New York: HarperBusiness.

Leamnson, R. (1999). *Thinking about teaching and learning: Developing habits of learning with first year college and university students.* Sterling, VA: Stylus.

LeDoux, J. (2002). *Synaptic self: How our brains become who we are.* New York: Viking Press.

Marshall, S. P. (2006). *The power to transform: Leadership that brings learning and schooling to life.* San Francisco: Jossey-Bass.

MacKenzie, G. (1998). *Orbiting the giant hairball: A corporate fool's guide to surviving with grace.* New York: Viking Press.

Michalko, M. (2006). *Thinkertoys: A handbook of creative-thinking techniques.* Berkeley, CA: Ten Speed Press.

Oshry, B. (1995). *Seeing systems: Unlocking the mysteries of organizational life.* San Francisco: Berret-Koehler.

Palmer, P. (1999). *The courage to teach.* San Francisco: Jossey-Bass.

Pearce, T. (2003). *Leading out loud: Inspiring change through authentic communication.* San Francisco: Jossey-Bass.

Pink, D. H. (2005). *A whole new mind: Why right-brainers will rule the future.* New York: Riverhead Books.

Pinker, S. (1997). *How the mind works.* New York: Norton.

Quinn, R. E. (1996). *Deep change: Discovering the leader within.* San Francisco: Jossey-Bass.

Racosky, R. J. (2003). *Go vertical! Life has no ceiling.* Boulder, CO: RocketFuel Publishing.

Ratey, J. J. (2001). *A user's guide to the brain.* New York: Pantheon Books.

Restak, R. (2001). *Mozart's brain and the fighter pilot: Unleashing your brain's potential.* New York: Three Rivers Press.

Rose, S. (2005). *The future of the brain.* New York: Oxford University Press.

Scharmer, C. O. (2007). *Theory U: Leading from the future as it emerges.* Cambridge, MA: Society for Organizational Learning.

Schultz, H., & Yang, D. J. (1997). *Pour your heart into it: How Starbucks built a company one cup at a time.* New York: Hyperion.

Senge, P., Ross, R., Smith, B., Roberts, C., & Kleiner, A. (1994). *The fifth discipline fieldbook: Strategies and tools for building a learning organization.* New York: Doubleday.

Tharp, T. (2003). *The creative habit: Learn it and use it for life.* New York: Simon & Schuster.

Tomlinson, C. A., & Allen, S. D. (2000). *Leadership for differentiating schools and classrooms.* Alexandria, VA: Association for Supervision and Curriculum Development.

Vaill, P. B. (1996). *Learning as a way of being: Strategies for survival in a world of permanent white water.* San Francisco: Jossey-Bass.

Wheatley, M. J., & Kellner-Rogers, M. (1996). *A simpler way.* San Francisco: Berrett-Koehler.

Zander, R. S., & Zander, B. (2000). *The art of possibility.* New York: Penguin Books.

Zemelman, S., Daniels, H., & Hyde, A. (2005). *Best practice: Today's standard for teaching and learning in America's schools.* Portsmouth, NH: Heinemann.

References

Andreasen, N. C. (2005). *The creating brain: The neuroscience of genius.* New York: Dana Press.

Arthur, W. B., Jaworski, J., & Scharmer, O. (2007). Unpublished slide. Generon Consulting: Cambridge, MA.

Baldwin, C. (1994). *Calling the circle: The first and future culture.* New York: Bantam Books.

Begley, S. (2007). *Train your mind, change your brain: How a new science reveals our extraordinary power to transform ourselves.* New York: Ballantine Books.

Bertalanffy, L. von. (1968). *General system theory: Foundations, development, applications.* New York: Braziller.

Bertalanffy, L. von, as quoted by Jan Kamaryt. (1973). From science to meta-science and philosophy. In Gray, W. & Rizzo, N. D. (Eds.), *Unity through diversity* (p. 77). New York: Gordon and Breach.

Brown, J., Isaacs, D., & the World Café. (2005). *The World Café: Shaping our futures through conversations that matter.* San Francisco: Berrett-Koehler.

Caine, G., & Caine, R. N. (2001). *The brain, education, and the competitive edge.* Lanham, MD: Scarecrow Press.

Caine, R. N. (in press). How neuroscience informs our teaching of elementary students. In C. Block, S. Parris, & P. Afflerbach (Eds.), *Comprehension instruction* (2nd ed.). New York: Guilford Press.

Caine, R. N., & Caine, G. (1991). *Making connections: Teaching and the human brain.* Alexandria, VA: Association for Supervision and Curriculum Development.

Caine, R. N., Caine, G., McClintic, C., & Klimek, K. (2004). *12 brain/mind learning principles in action: The fieldbook for making connections, teaching, and the human brain.* Thousand Oaks, CA: Corwin Press.

Cooperrider, D. L., & Srivastava, S. (1987). Appreciative inquiry in organizational life. *Research in Organizational Change and Development, 1,* 129–169.

Cooperrider, D., & Whitney, D. (2005). *Appreciative inquiry: A positive revolution in change.* San Francisco: Berrett-Koehler.

Cooperrider, D., Whitney, D., & Stavros, J. (2003). *Appreciative inquiry handbook.* San Francisco: Berrett-Koehler.

Edwards, T. (2007). Shaping organizational futures through generative leadership. *Leadership Abstracts, 20*(2), 1–4.

Forrester, J. W. (1989). *The beginning of system dynamics.* Retrieved November 21, 2007, from http://sysdyn.clexchange.org/sdep/papers/D-4165-1.pdf

Forrester, J. W. (1996). System dynamics and K–12 teachers. *Sloan School Monograph,* D-4665-4. (Available at http://sysdyn.clexchange.org/sdep/papers/D-4665-4.pdf)

Fullan, M. (2005). *Leadership & sustainability: System thinkers in action.* Thousand Oaks, CA: Corwin Press.

Gardner, H. (1985). *The mind's new science: A history of the cognitive revolution.* New York: Basic Books.

Gardner, H. (1993). *The unschooled mind: How children think and how schools should teach.* New York: Basic Books.

Generon Consulting. (2005). *The change lab fieldbook.* Cambridge, MA: Author.

Gergen, K. J. (1978). Toward generative theory. *Journal of Personality and Social Psychology, 11,* 1344–1360.

Gibbs, J. (2001). *Tribes: A new way of learning and being together.* Windsor, CA: CenterSource Systems.

Goleman, D. (2006). *Social intelligence: The new science of human relationships.* New York: Bantam Dell.

Gopnik, A., Meltzoff, A. N., & Kuhl, P. K. (1999). *The scientist in the crib: Minds, brains, and how children learn.* New York: William Morrow.

Haidt, J. (2006). *The happiness hypothesis: Finding modern truth in ancient wisdom.* New York: Basic Books.

Hart, L. A. (1998). *Human brain and human learning.* Kent, WA: Books for Educators.

Havel, V. (1985). *The power of the powerless: Citizens against the state in Central-Eastern Europe* (J. Kean, Ed.). Armonk, NY: M. E. Sharpe.

Havel, V. (1985). The power of the powerless: *Citizens against the state in Central-Eastern Europe* (J. Kean, Ed.). Retrieved August 2005 from http://www.vaclavhavel.cz/index.php?sec=2&id=1.

Jensen, E. (1995). *Teaching with the Brain in Mind (2nd Ed.).* Alexandria, VA: ASCD.

Kolb, D. (1984). *Experiential learning: Experience as the source of learning and development.* Englewood Cliffs, NJ: Prentice Hall.

Miller, J. G. (1978). *Living systems.* New York: McGraw-Hill.

Miller, J. G., & Miller, J. L. (1997). *Applications of living systems theory.* Paper presented for the First International Electronic Seminar on Wholeness, December 1, 1996, to December 31, 1997. Retrieved November 21, 2007, from www.newciv.org/ISSS_Primer/asem05jm.html

National Research Council. (1999). *How People Learn: Brain, Mind, Experience, and School.* Washington, D.C.: National Academy Press.

Pert, C. (1997). *Molecules of emotion.* New York: Scribner.

Restak, R. (2003). *The new brain.* Emmaus, PA: Rodale Press.

Rizzolatti, G., & Craighero, L. (2004). The mirror neuron system. *Annual Reviews of Neuroscience, 27,* 169–192.

Scharmer, O. (2007). *Theory U: Leading from the future as it emerges.* Cambridge, MA: Society for Organizational Learning.

Senge, P. (1990). *The fifth discipline.* New York: Doubleday.

Senge, P., Cambron McCabe, N. H., Lucas, T., & Kleiner, A. (2000). *Schools that learn: A fifth discipline fieldbook for educators, parents, and everyone who cares about education.* New York: Doubleday.

Senge, P., Scharmer, C. O., Jaworski, J., & Flowers, B. S. (2004). *Presence: Human purpose and the field of the future.* Cambridge, MA: Society for Organizational Learning.

Sylwester, R. (2005). *How to explain a brain: An educator's handbook of brain terms and cognitive processes.* Thousand Oaks, CA: Corwin Press.

Watkins, J. M., & Mohr, B. J. (2001). *Appreciative inquiry: Change at the speed of imagination.* San Francisco: Jossey-Bass/Pfeiffer.

Wheatley, M. J. (1992). *Leadership and the new science: Discovering order in a chaotic world.* San Francisco: Berrett-Koehler.

Wheatley, M. J. (2002). *Turning to one another: Simple conversations to restore hope to the future.* San Francisco: Berrett-Koehler.

Wheatley, M. J. (2005). *Finding our way: Leadership for an uncertain time.* San Francisco: Berrett-Koehler.

Whitney, D., Trosten-Bloom, A., Cherney, J., & Fry, R. (2004). *Appreciative teambuilding: Positive questions to bring out the best of your team.* Lincoln, NE: iUniverse.

Zull, J. E. (2002). *The art of changing the brain: Enriching teaching by exploring the biology of learning.* Sterling, VA: Stylus.

Index